Dave Clark has been equipping fathers for over two decades. He has inspired thousands through his speaking and teaching. Dave's work and the non-profit, The Father's Cry, has had international influence as he has traveled the globe sharing the "secrets of effective fathers". I can assure you Dave and his family are committed to excellence, but what distinguishes him is his willingness to be honest about his shortcomings and challenges, and with integrity, work through those issues. Dave's book, The Father's Cry, is a quick read, full of engaging stories and when you reflect on his insights, you will be stirred to make fathering a top priority in your life. I heartily recommend his book to you.

-Ken R Canfield PhD.
Founder of the National Center for Fathering

DAVE CLARK

The Father's Cry

A STORY OF HEALING
& FAMILY RESTORATION

Copyright © 2021 by Dave Clark

Published by Clay Bridges in Houston, TX

www.ClayBridgesPress.com

All rights reserved. No part of this publication may be reproduced, stored in a retrieval system, or transmitted in any form by any means, electronic, mechanical, photocopy, recording, or otherwise, with the prior permission of the publisher, except as provided for by USA copyright law.

All statistics and research done and used by permission of © 2021 The National Center for Public Policy Research Washington, DC.

ISBN: 978-1-953300-57-7
eISBN: 978-1-953300-59-1

Contents

Acknowledgments 7
Foreword 9
More Than an Introduction 13
Preface   Who is this Guy? 19
Chapter 1   The Longest Ride of My Life 25
Chapter 2   What an Awful Christmas 29
Chapter 3   It Is All on Me 33
Chapter 4   We Seemed Just Like Other Families 37
Chapter 5   Sports, Church, Work, and Hormones 42
Chapter 6   Can I Fill It with Up Regular or Premium Gas? 47
Chapter 7   Life Took a Major Turn 51
Chapter 8   Leaving and Starting on My Terms 61
Chapter 9   A Lucky Break or God? 67
Chapter 10 It Seemed Like God 72
Chapter 11 I Finally Got a Rhythm 78
Chapter 12 Maybe Foreshadowing. But Maybe God After All 84
Chapter 13 When Does This Ever Get Better? 95
Chapter 14 Life after Jail 103
Chapter 15 Kim's Chapter 117
Chapter 16 The Toolbox 126
Chapter 17 The Course 138
Chapter 18 Final Thoughts 206

Acknowledgments

I want to acknowledge Dr. Ken Canfield, author of "The Seven Secrets of Effective Fathers" and numerous books on fathering. Dr. Ken Canfield is a worldwide respected leader and scholar who has committed his life to strengthening fathers and families. He founded the National Center for Fathering (fathers.com) and is the respected champion for fathers. I have taken Ken Canfield's book and trained men across the United States, Belarus, seven African countries, United Arab Emirates, and Pakistan. I was privileged to attend a Master Trainer's Course in the '90s at the National Center for Fathering under the direction of Ron Nichols. It was during this three-day encounter that I embraced the "The Seven Secrets of Effective Fathers" program. Ron never knew the impact he made on my life in extending grace to me for three days in his class and guiding me through my self-awareness of fatherhood. The Seven Secrets has changed everything about my life as a father and husband. The true fathering champions for fatherhood have changed thousands of marriages, fathers, families, communities, and nations that have witnessed their heart of fathering.

I would like to acknowledge all the past and present great men and women on staff at the National Center for Fathering (fathers.com). Through the years, this staff influenced my purpose in training men to become effective fathers. It gave me the tools I needed for my fathering toolbox. My family and I will be eternally grateful.

A special thank-you to Betty Swann of Betty Swann Ministries for speaking into my life and insisting my voice and message were important for fathers and families as we traveled across the world. I would also like to thank my brother and his wife, Steve and Becca Clark, for reading and editing the book. To my big brother Ron for being a great big brother while growing up and demonstrating perseverance. A special thank you to Dana Taylor for navigating me through a time of great sadness and finding a safe ground in being a healthy man, father, and husband. For my colleague, Kudzai Shoko, for his encouragement with me training fathers in Africa and the Middle East. There were many men, such as Rick Trafton, who walked with me in the worst times of my life and encouraged me not to give up on the Father or myself.

Finally, I would like to acknowledge my dad for all the reasons he and I know from the many hours we worked with one another and the last years walking alongside his life. For Kim, who re-read, edited, and was very kind in her many suggestions in writing the story. In so many ways, my story is her story. For my two sons Braden and Casey. I can only say I wished I had it to do over again. Despite the many flaws of being your father, both of you have become everything I dreamed of becoming, remarkable men.

"Old man take a look at my life - I'm a lot like you."

By Casey Clark

Foreword

It is my honor to write the foreword to my father's book. The Title of the foreword comes from a song by Neil Young. "Old Man" is not meant as an insult; instead, it is a song of common ground. I've known this song for at least twenty years now and have sung it for as many years. I am 40 years old, the young man singing to the old. I am the son saying to the father, "I'm not so different than you, you know." "Look into my eyes. You can tell it's true." And it is true. Fathers, your children are more of you than you sometimes care to know.

My father is the man writing this book. My mother is the woman who shares in this mission -- this fatherhood mission. I am the younger son who stayed home while his older brother raised hell. One of the more memorable phrases of my youth was my father saying to me, "For all, we know your brother could be lying dead in a gutter somewhere." Though there was a certain amount of truth to this, such words from a father don't exactly inspire hope in a kid.

Most of my childhood was a lesson in duality. There was the outer image, the shell that was our family: the churchgoing, community-involved, hard-working, American family stuff. Then there was the private reality, the inner sanctum of conflict. There's always dirty laundry that no one wants to air in public. And naturally so. But what about when you need help? To whom do you turn when nothing is going right? Here is where the public Clark family and the private Clark family clashed. The private issues of brokenness, rebellion, disrespect (and the list goes on) had to be acknowledged.

But when my family turned to (our) church, there was no one there who understood. Sure, there were prayers passed around, like "Thank you, Jesus, that's not my family," and "We just pray that Brady stops wearing baggy clothes and listening to evil music." Totally missing the point. When our family hit bottom, Sunday school Christian morality didn't cut it anymore. This was evident to every one of us, Dave, Kim, Brady, and Casey. Though it would take time and pain to learn, the outer image meant nothing. The real tragedy was that a father and son hated each other precisely for who they were. And they were remarkably alike.

I can't say I ever hated my father. Perhaps it is because we are different enough. My brother and my dad are similar, and this is precisely why they butted heads. My brother was rebellious because my father taught him and drove him to be so. While operating simultaneously in fear and hope, my dad was trying to involve himself and shape my brother so that Brady succeeded where he did not. When Brady did not live up to expectations on the soccer field or in the classroom, my dad's disappointment was audible and tangible. Most of the time, I caught his spit, wind, and fury in the backseat beside my brother. I was not often the object of his fire, and so I did not hate my father. But I feared him.

Though I have no children of my own, I understand now more than ever the reasons why fathers and mothers put so much pressure on children. Most of the time, it is for a child's benefit. The world is not fair. You don't always get what you want. Share. Say, "Thank you." Make good grades. Success in this world takes hard work. As the shepherd of his family, the father naturally nurtures and prepares his children for the realities that life holds.

But expectations are always beholden to disappointment. When a child doesn't do well in school or forgets to take out the trash, a parent rightly expresses disapproval. But when a child feels he/she can never live up to a parent's expectations, then maybe there is a disconnect. A parent may feel justified in putting pressure on his child, but a child may end up feeling loved conditionally. You may tell them differently, but in my experience, a kid is watching and learning even when you're not trying to teach. This was the case with my family. Somehow along the way, the disconnect between my father and brother had grown to a gulf. How was the gulf healed? Not by a church, but by the father himself. My dad had to be practically hit over the head a couple of times to wake up, but our family's restoration happened to begin when a father was himself healed. Only then could the son come home because he no longer recognized the hate that had been in his eye.

I now feel that there is nothing that would separate me from the love of my parents. This, I think, is a commendable example of God's love, The Love.

I think it could have easily gone the other way. I mean, the disconnect could still be there, like it is for a lot of families. But the message of hope is this: Our family was hopeless, and here I am writing about how it worked out, despite our low points. Not that there won't be new low points as the next Clark generation emerges, but by the pure grace of God, it will be built on a strong foundation.

Casey Clark, Son, and Member of The Father's Cry Ministry

More Than an Introduction

More than 20 million children live in a home without the physical presence of a father. Millions more have dads who are physically present but emotionally absent. If fatherlessness could be classified as a disease, it would be an epidemic worthy of attention as a worldwide emergency. The impact of fatherlessness can be seen in our homes, schools, and prisons. In short, fatherlessness can be associated with almost every societal ill facing our world's children. According to 72.2% of the U.S. population, fatherlessness is the most significant family or social problem facing America. The statistics regarding fathering are staggering. Worldwide, father-absent statistics vary from culture, country, statistical methodology, and the lack of information. Without any hesitation, the conclusions of the world trend parallel with fatherlessness in the United States. Many refer to our time as the Fatherless Generation. My point, dads are abandoning kids.

As you review the Table of Contents of this book on a website or while standing in a local bookstore or at an airport bookstand waiting for a flight, you may be trying to determine whether this book is worth the read.

One decision has been made in your mind.

There is some question lingering within you about fatherhood.

Maybe I can help clarify any issues about fatherhood? I don't know about you, but I had purchased too many books that later hit the trash can when I realized the book is not what I expected.

Honestly, this book is not written to be a ten-point self-help guide on how to be a good dad. There are plenty of "how-to" books on bookstore shelves, and this book will never fit that category. This story is about how one man, who seemed to have everything going his way, had a catastrophic issue take place in his marriage and home. The catastrophe seemed related to a lack of priorities regarding family and fatherhood. My story will give you an honest and personal fatherhood journey that all fathers walk. My family's general opinion is that our family struggle to bring healing is probably not an exception but today's norm in most societies worldwide. More than one-half of the marriages in my country fail. We are at epidemic rates for kids living without a dad or living with a second dad due to divorce or abandonment. In the United States alone, almost 24.1 million children (33%) live absent from their biological father. All the fatherhood statistics would be higher in third-world countries if statistical studies were available.

This book does not intend to judge you as a father in your fathering journey. However, it will contain information based on Ken Canfield's "The Seven Secrets of Effective Fathers" to guide you in your fatherhood journey. Before this is all over, you and I will be sitting in my fatherhood course together. The course will be real and authentic, talking about what it takes to be an effective father. I, too, have attended a similar course in incredible pain, lacking hope and looking for solutions. It seemed I failed in my role of being a good husband and father. For the man picking up this book, I am hopeful one of my stories resonates with you, so it will help you find answers to some of your questions about fatherhood. Perhaps, the book will challenge you to consider making some changes in how you think or behave as a father. It may challenge you to release or let go of some anger and unforgiveness in your life reflected as a father. So, continue with me as I tell my story. The questions you may have asked regarding a troubled son or daughter, or a troubled marriage, might find an answer during our journey together. I hope by me sharing the guts of my life, you will be able to trust me in the direction I am suggesting to you. I think you will find that what I say will be safe and worth every minute of your time. This story is not a religious book full of flowery spiritual words like those you might have already tried to read and ended up putting down. However, a significant part of being an effective father is spiritual in nature.

I have intentionally chosen not to glamorize any of my stories because it would be misleading about who I was and who I am. It is like putting on our best Sunday clothes and polishing our shoes on Saturday night for church the next day. Like me, many of us may sit in church or a mosque or synagogue, looking our best only to hide our pain and sadness. I promised myself that if I ever wrote a book, it would be real and authentic. As I listen to men talk about their marriage or fathering problems, they tell me just be honest with them or, as they say, "Just say it, don't B.S. me." If nothing else, my family will see me in ways I have failed to talk about in our life. Perhaps this book is written as much for me as it is for you.

Many fathering stories end in horror. Your story could include your son or daughter's unexpected death, drug overdose, pregnancy, suicide, weapons, jail, gangs, or leaving home, never to be seen or heard from again. Maybe that home was absent of joy, happiness, laughter, and financial security. In my case, Brady was my fifteen-year-old eldest son who got into the world of drugs, tattoos, body piercings, and trouble with the police. My wife and I decided that he had to either play by our family rules or leave our home. He gladly left a house of condemnation and stress. The short version of the story is Brady got kicked out of high school his senior year. He lived on the streets, stealing and doing drugs, and often wound up in the local city jail only to progress to county jail on charges of burglary of a habitation and weapons. In other countries, he would have just gone to jail. In America, there are several levels of jails like a town, region, and state jail system or what many refer to as a province. Then the bigger jails are the state jails and federal prison system. Regardless of the facility, he understood a jail cell and bars. His younger brother, Casey, was a smart and talented kid like his brother but learned to avoid the verbal onslaught in our home by keeping his mouth shut. He soon realized that taking cover or having diversions became essential to his immediate survival.

To say it mildly, I had enough guilt, shame, hurt, and disappointments to fill up any football stadium, soccer pitch, or cricket stadium. But what if you could risk journeying with me and read my family's story? We just might have a lot in common. Come with me as we travel through our life experiences and then answer the question: What do I need to do differently? How can I restore a failed relationship with my children or my dad? Or simply, what can I do better as a father and as a husband? I hope you will read many things in this book that will validate your fathering efforts. On the flipside is the statement, "I never knew about that…no one ever told me." You might not have experienced a tragedy with a daughter or son and cannot identify with some of this story. However, my bet is there will be a time at work that a co-worker will ask you for a cup of coffee or tea during your break time. It is when you ask, "How are things?" that the bottom of the bucket falls out from a father whose home and family seem to have collapsed. He may be at that point where he cannot even cry anymore.

The towns you and I grew up in will be different. Our life experiences could be very similar but different. Our problems with our marriage or kids are very similar but different. As I travel across the world, it is not unusual to sit in a remote African village or a local coffee shop in Pakistan talking to men about fathering. As I sit in my local coffee shop, it is easy to hear men talk about their kids and wives. I find without exception, we all share the same issues with fatherhood. We listen to men who sit in tears, talking about how, as a little boy or teenager, his father would hit him or curse him and call him names and even abandon the family. We hear men talk about their wives who have left their marriage after discovering their husbands have had multiple affairs with other women. We listen to men talk about never wanting a kid when faced with an unexpected pregnancy. As I sit in groups of men, I can always see the one man sitting in total shock because of what he is hearing. This man can't relate because he had a great dad and home. Usually, his question is, how can he help other children without fathers? How can he help other fathers? I want you to know whatever your issues may be in your fatherhood journey; this book will give you answers to being an "Effective Father." This book offers you tools to help the next guy sitting in the break room at work, pouring out his grief that his son or daughter left home the night before.

More Than an Introduction

You may be tired of picking up the same type of books looking for answers or solutions, only to find they seem to say the same things with some variations. This book will lean toward being a bit raw, but I think I can talk about fathering better than most men writing about this topic. I believe few men have my experience in meeting fathers across the world over the past twenty years. I have sat with men from remote towns in Belarus to villages in Africa or home churches in Pakistan or sitting in my living room in Texas. I know I am not wrong or off-target. I think I have seen, heard, and witnessed more about everyday father struggles than most men today. For me, fathering is not an academic idea but a real issue in everyday homes across the world.

I would like to add a final word on reading this book. We often pick up books, and we don't know what direction the book is leading us. I know I am terrible about reading ahead, trying to get an idea of what is next or where a story may be going. I am horrible when watching a movie on my DVD player or some other media platform. If I am bored or just anxious about the next scene, I tend to jump ahead and get a preview.

Before you do that, let me explain how this will read. I will take you into my personal stories and my struggles of being a son, husband, and father. My attempt in this style of writing is to give you a glimpse into my family. I hope there are parts of my story where we will have some things in common. I will work hard in using terms that are familiar to all of us but know I will fail in some of my chapters. We may use different definitions of God on how we view our spiritual formation and framework. I firmly believe we all share a common ground of influencing and connecting our children's spiritual needs with our faith beliefs. I think we all want our children to experience the spiritual emotion of our faiths. Throughout my stories, I will share the impact of my spiritual experiences on my life from a little boy to a grown man. I hope you can look past our cultural and other differences and read my heart in what I mean about fathering.

The book will take on a more conversational tone between us. I don't think I ever picked up a book, and it told me upfront how it will read. Some authors seemed to leave it up to you to figure it out. With me, I become impatient and just walk away from it. My wife will just dust around it on the coffee table, occasionally asking me if

I am ever going to finish that book. I am not saying that has always worked out well for me because I missed some opportunities that I needed to hear. At the end of the book, you and I will dig deeper into father issues and find answers through a course I teach worldwide.

My real wish is that you and I could get away for a few days just talking about our fathering stories letting our guards down, just being real and honest. It would be a lot easier. My idea would be for us to be in a remote mountain area in front of a fire, trying to sort some things out as friends.

I know we are not able to sit with each other while we study this book. Like many conversations, there are times you might get offended, misunderstood, and walk away from it. It might even get a little confrontational. If that happens, I would normally follow you and probably confront you, asking what's going on? Maybe I hit a raw nerve, and you want to continue to leave it buried. You can do that with me in this story. But I would urge you to let me follow you, and we can continue the talk together.

Preface

Who is this Guy?

This story is about a man who thought of himself as a pretty good guy, especially by many standards in today's world. If you were to ask people in the "who's who" in almost every West Texas town in the state, they would recognize the name and most likely say, "He is a great guy."

He was about everything a man would dream of being in terms of success. He was a top executive, a Senior Vice-President, in one of the largest hospital systems in the Southwest United States. He served on numerous non-profit community boards raising hundreds of thousands of dollars for worthy community benefits and serving local and state boards. Every time you turned around, he was on television, in the newspaper, or featured in various news and magazine articles. He was a frequent speaker at state and national health conventions around the United States. This guy was great. He developed all kinds of health programs that impacted the lives of patients and families for decades. It was unbelievable all he had accomplished in a career. With his energy level and stamina, his reputation was, "If you need something done, just call Dave. He will tell you straight and blunt." To beat that, he was married to a pretty petite blonde who was incredible. Together, they had two great sons. This family seemed to look like that perfect family you might see on a television show. If that were not enough, this guy would be the first to help the homeless or a family deprived of food or resources. He was there for anyone who had a need. He served at his local church as a Sunday school teacher and served as a youth sponsor. This guy was an action guy and looked so natural in all his leadership positions. But as this story will tell, he had all the right intentions but failed in one of the most critical aspects of the family.

Hi, my name is Dave Clark, and this is a story about my struggles as a father and husband.

As you grew up, perhaps like me, you may have dreamed about getting married and having a family. You might have thought about that perfect girl or that ideal family out on vacation at a lake or a beach running and laughing and cooking over a fire. In that imagined place, life is great. You have a happy family.

Well, my story didn't quite go that way, not by my design but by a lack of priorities, skills, and knowledge. I actually find most men struggle with the same issues of "how." Mine is an ugly story about how life, work, and public demand seemed to pull me away from the very thing I thought I held of great value. Over years of living with family turmoil and ultimately traveling the globe, I realize my story is not much different from many men.

I simply decided to expose our family's deepest secrets so that men might find an avenue for self-healing and family restoration.

As with other books you may have read, I hope you continue to read my story. I hope you hesitate a little longer before putting it on that coffee table with other unread books, thinking it does not apply to your life. I hope my story will touch a feeling or emotion tucked away due to a hurt caused by a father's word or action. I will refer to this as a father hurt or father wound.

So, would you take a risk and read a little bit more with me?

This story is not just about me but my family. I am not sure when the story started because it seemed gradual. In looking back in time, the hurts I am responsible for probably began with my older son as early as four years old on a soccer field, screaming at him when he missed a shot four feet from the goal. In rediscovering my past, my father hurts probably started as early as my years in junior high school—more on that to come.

Who is this Guy?

You may look at the book title or skip through the book's Introduction and decide this book doesn't fit your life because you feel OK about being a dad. You may think the book does not affect you because your kids are grown and gone. Or you may be the father who says, "I am doing OK as a father." I do respect those comments, but I am going to challenge you to keep reading. My response to you is I never intended to be a lousy father, but I was. I never intended to write a book or travel the globe encouraging men to be educated on fatherhood, but I did. When I begin teaching a fatherhood class, I ask men one simple question. How many of you have passed your fatherhood class? I get this blank look as I communicate that none of us have been told or educated on being an Effective Father. The fact of the matter is, we did what we saw or heard our dad or our uncle, granddad, or big brother do growing up. No one taught us how to be a father.

I'll tell you what I tell men everywhere I travel - I had a good dad. He didn't molest me or lock me up in a closet naked and bruised. I will give him credit for giving it a great effort. But the fact of the matter is that he often screamed and belittled me or whipped me and hurt me along with my other two brothers. His behavior didn't seem out of the ordinary for him because of the era he grew up as a boy and man. After all, do as you see. I vowed many times not to do the things my dad did to me, but I found myself doing just that with my sons.

I realize the hurts that my dad placed on my little boy soul hung on to be my big boy hurts. I became a master of hiding my hurts, and by every glance, I was a good and successful man.

The fact is I became a dad who had anger issues and erratic behaviors and was afraid of failure. I discover many men often have problems with their fathers that stop them from really being wonderful husbands and dads and being free from their hurt. At 96, my dad was soft, loving, and had come to grips with his good, bad, and ugly self and resolved any issues he had with my two brothers and me before he died. He became verbally and physically very loving, and at death, my brothers and I stood at his grave with resolved love and respect for my dad. In the end, he left a positive legacy for generations of Clark men.

If you placed yourself in the category of "been there and done that but now I am a granddad," or you have a poor relationship with your grown children, then I have a challenge for you. What if you could become an even greater granddad? A good question to ask right here is what stopped you from being everything you wanted in a dad or husband. I will answer the question for myself: It was hurt. The next question is, what are you doing about it? I know those words might seem a little threatening. My response to that question is I really didn't think I needed to do much about it. The fact of the matter is I didn't understand the "cause and effect" of being hurt.

You see, this story is for all of us, no matter our age or if you are a good dad or not. The reality is we never stop being a father. The Number One audience I seem to address is older men experiencing broken relationships with their grown kids. It seems they can't find a way to make things OK again from the years of harsh words or discipline. Then there are the younger men who have no desire to do what their dad did to them. These men want to know how to do things better as a father and husband. It is my firm belief that we have become accustomed to what I call "pulling a mask" over our face. We are used to acting the way we do to the point that we can feel OK about "ourselves." My question is, what would we look like or be like if we could pull that mask off and see another guy?" I always thought to myself, "What is holding me back from really being great…not just good but great?" I know that I can be a lot better because I find myself wondering what the heck just happened or what just came flying out of my mouth, or I asked myself, "Where did that come from!?" Sometimes I would walk away and say, "Clark, you're better than that!"

You see, I am not a psychologist, counselor, book writer, or any person like that. I am just a retired healthcare consultant. I am a guy at 72 trying to be an effective father, grandfather and desperately loving my wife. I bet I am a lot like you working to have enough money for retirement, pay all my bills, and being happy. Along with most guys, I would say I am probably OK. But I know I can be more than what I am or appear to be. I am better than just being OK. Well, guys, this is a lot about how I worked behind a mask of hurts, disappointments, and failures. I never learned how to talk about those faults or share them for fear of being judged or viewed as weak and a failure. It is sort of like that dad saying to the little boy, "Don't cry, men don't cry." Guess what? We do when no one is looking. Thus, the name for our ministry, "The Father's Cry."

Look, I don't want to push you down that path of doom or sadness and no joy because, in the midst of this, I was successful, and life was not all disappointments. I certainly had my share of success mixed with the ugly. I wasn't on the edge of suicide but was very defeated.

I hope you will read further in the story and find your way through dropping your mask and being free in yourself. I hope you might see some of you in me and how we could resolve some of our issues through the stories. Don't get me wrong. I am not proud of any of this. Shame, embarrassment, failure, ego, and secrets defined me in many ways. Those were just a few descriptions I could tattoo on my forehead, and trust me, at any given time, there were more. As I tell men, you can probably still see the vomit stains on my back porch, trying to sort some of this out.

Chapter 1
The Longest Ride of My Life

I will never forget that night. It was Christmas Eve, and I remember that my younger son, Casey, and my wife, Kim, and I were traveling down the highway on a cold night with a drizzle in the air to see our oldest son. It was a night of all nights. I occasionally glance in the rearview mirror and see Casey just staring out the window in what might be a stare into nowhere. He sat with no emotion and life as this journey had taken a toll on him. As I looked at Kim, I saw a woman slumped in depression and almost a soulless body. She had lost weight and seemed to age beyond her years. There was no talking, not even the sound of a radio. I just remember the sound of the windshield wipers going back and forth. It was gut-wrenching. It had to be the longest ride we had taken of what was a fragmented and dysfunctional family – all resting on me. I felt responsible for the years of anger outbursts, not being at home enough, and certainly missing out on a fun and happy home. My faith told me that the responsibility of my family and kids rested on my shoulders.

I remember finally arriving and waiting in a lobby with many people going to the same place. As best as we could muster, we had clean clothes, nice clothes, and we still stood out as being different. There we stood with a room full of Hispanics and African Americans and what I might refer to as poor white people. Yet, in our differences in clothes, social status, money, homes, life, and work, we had one thing in common. We were all waiting to go into the county jail to see our sons. You see, after years of being on the street, gangs, drugs, sex, and being homeless, he is arrested on charges of burglary of a habitation and weapons possession. I still couldn't get that in my head. My oldest son, a charged felon. A kid who got expelled his senior year of high school after I told him to leave my house at sixteen for being totally out of control.

The elevator opened. A man came out of the elevator and said we could go up in groups, and we squeezed into the elevator. I will never forget looking down, and a small Hispanic kid was holding his mom's hands just staring at me. I couldn't say anything but just looked away and waited for the elevator door to open. Funny, the ride up the elevator was only one floor. That ride seemed to take an eternity. It stopped, and the door opened to a large room full of plastic booths. There stood an officer with a stomach hanging over his belt and in a big gruff voice saying choose a glass booth, and we had ten minutes to talk. He seemed like he hated life and was pissed for working on Christmas Eve. I suddenly had a focus to point my anger. As I walked by him, I thought that you could have some sensitivity that we were there on Christmas Eve visiting our kid. After all, you should care. As I looked up, Kim and Casey were walking ahead toward a vacant booth. I realized I got so caught up in my anger and fear instead of being a supportive dad or husband during one of the greatest hurts in our family.

The big door behind the booths opened, and everyone was standing looking for a dad, brother, or a son, and then there he was. He wore orange jail coveralls and all his hair cut. He looked thirteen when, in effect, he was eighteen. I remember thinking Kim should talk because of our limited visitation time limit. As bad as I wanted to cry and call out, anger and shame stopped me. Somewhere in my head were childhood voices going off to be tough, don't cry, be a man, and stand straight. All the things a little boy hears growing up, not having a great image of himself, was screaming at me.

Sure enough, he sat down and lit up when he saw his mom. He ignored me as though I was a speck of dust in the universe. Casey got up close to his mom, and I just remember Casey looked like he was in total shock. I remember looking at Casey in what seemed to him, figuring out how to cry and smile at the same time. After all, none of this is what he had bargained for being a kid in middle school, trying to get through the pain of growing up. I had not prepared him for what he was going to see or what to expect. I knew what to expect from dealing with healthcare issues in local jails. I was clueless because I was so self-centered on myself and not on Kim and Casey.

The time came when Kim handed me the phone, and Brady just literally screamed at me. His first words were that the guards had told him that I arranged to get his bail raised, and he wouldn't be there if it weren't for me. He yelled at me that he would have been home for Christmas if not for me. Brady said that the guards told him I had got to the judge and had his bail raised another fifty-thousand dollars, which meant he would stay till his court hearing in January. Of course, I said I didn't have that kind of power, and he was wrong. He said a few more things to Casey that was a total blur to me, and then the jail alarm sounded that it was time to leave. I remember Kim followed him out of the room with her red bloodshot eyes till the door closed, and he was gone. I have no memory of the ride home, as it was a big blur.

Brady was correct. The fact was I had appealed to the District Judge, whom I knew from past civic fundraisers. I had written him a letter asking that he increase Brady's bail so his friends could not raise the money to get him out. One day my brother called me and said, "Hey, Justin (his son and my nephew) just called him. He said he was at a local fast-food restaurant getting lunch, and there were a bunch of local kids trying to raise money for Brady. They were going table to table asking for donations." The fact was many of his friends had raised the cash to get him out on bail, and I had to stop it. Somehow, I knew I would lose him to that world of kids roaming and living on the streets. His friends had even robbed our home to sell garage items to help him make a jail bond.

At that time of my career, I knew many judges and law enforcement officers in a large twenty-six-county area. That area was more extensive than many countries in the world. I directed an Emergency Medical System, and I had frequent meetings with law enforcement staff regarding training and education. Yes, I knew the District Judge who would preside over his court hearing. He was mean, fair, a Christian but had no tolerance toward gangster punk kids. That would be my kid. Nonetheless, I explained to the judge that Brady was a good kid, and we were a good family who took some wrong turns along the way. "I" had taken some wrong turns along the way.

How do you have a Christmas without your son being home? How do we tell family, people at work, and friends that Brady was in jail facing serious crimes? Life could not have been any worse. There was no hope, little love, emptiness, a home void of life, and a loveless bed I shared with my wife, a younger son who was hurt, embarrassed, ashamed, and angry.

I remember sitting in the living room in front of the Christmas tree, asking the question, "How did I get here?" More in-depth and nonverbal conversations seem to always lead to the past.

Chapter 2
What an Awful Christmas

It seems in a crisis that we want to blame someone or make others accountable for our mistakes. I am probably no different. Later as I grew up, I had to admit my parents never physically abused me as we know it today. I wanted to blame my dad for being an angry man, and what seemed like this ugly madman in him was jumping all over our house, and no one had control. I knew that wasn't right. The fact of the matter is my dad did what his father did and what he saw, heard, and felt at night when he went to bed as a little boy and young man. I've thought and cried some nights thinking of what may have been Dad's night-time feelings and thoughts.

I can't imagine the thoughts of that little boy as he laid next to his little brother in the bed they shared. It seemed that the images of what my dad saw his father do and say and feel simply got transferred into my head. Later in life, it would anger me when my dad and I would talk about some of these issues, and he would say, "I just did what I saw and heard my father do." While there was a lot of truth about that, I knew that wasn't entirely right. It might have been right for him, and that is all he could do or say, but it still left a hole in me full of anger. I often travel long hours in airplanes to fathering conferences across the world. I think somewhere between 20,000 feet and 30,000 feet in the dark of night on a trip to Africa, I forgave him entirely. He was right. He did what he knew to do. I knew for me to be emotionally healthy that I had to let go of the pain that hurt me.

I remember on that late-night plane trip to Kenya when all the lights were low and passengers asleep, I opened my briefcase and began to write:

Dad,

"I know as a boy growing up that you did what you saw and heard from granddaddy. I know you acted out that hurt that scared you because you didn't know any better. I know you walked in a lot of shame and hurt and fear. I know you lived in a time of life where you never talked about these things. I know, as the first child, you felt a big responsibility of taking care of your brother and sisters.

I remember on one of our Saturday morning trips to the bank and supermarket. You told me the story of your dad driving you to the edge of town when you had to report to the Army Air Corp in World War II. You said it was the week you were supposed to report to the army base in San Antonio, Texas. I remember you looking out the car window, sort of choking on some of your words when you told me granddaddy pulled the car over to the edge of the road. It was there he told you it was time to get out and hitchhike to report to the base. Gosh, that was at least a 12-hour drive.

I remember glancing over in the front seat and caught you, wiping a tear off your cheek. You paused, and then you said how scared you were at that moment. You said granddaddy looked over at you and said it is now time - you're on your own now, and you're a man. He said, Good luck, and then you watched your dad turn and drive home. I remember you telling me how alone and abandoned you felt that day. There were no hugs.

Dad, I know you did your very best. I know more than anyone that you were a son too. I know you did not wake up every day while I was growing up saying you would hurt me. But you did. Dad, I can't hold those hurts against you anymore. I release you, dad, from that hurt, fear, shame, and disappointment you passed down to me. I know we have talked about this a few times in the past few years. I just wanted to put a final closure to it because I never want to regret anything between us when you die.

Now, "Dad, I release you from all the pain I felt from you."

"God, I release my hurts to you."

(And I did, as dad died in 2018).

It was the next morning after the trip to the jail, Christmas day.

For the life of me, Christmas day was a blur. We have a tradition that on Christmas morning, Kim and I would get up and get breakfast ready to cook. We would turn on all the lights and get ready for two blurry-eyed boys to come down the stairs to see what Santa had left. It was a great picture, even for the dog waiting patiently with her best friends at the top of the stairs.

There stood Casey and the dog, waiting to come down the stairs. There was a significant vacancy at the top of the stairs that Christmas morning. The enthusiasm was barely visible as we tried to make the best of a day we all wanted to avoid. In the midst of that morning, we were determined not to let Brady's absence ruin everything about Casey's teen years at home. We were just hoping we could get only through the day amid our disappointments. After all, we were not going to allow many friends or family into our world of pain.

I am sure Casey got some neat stuff that Christmas. We would have made sure he got what he wished despite the confusion of our home. We ate the traditional cherry coffee cake, peppered bacon with scrambled eggs, cold milk, and a late lunch. For sure, no one was coming to our house because the effort for me to smile and just breathe was too hard. I could've eaten out of the trashcan that day for all that mattered. I don't remember anything about lunch or anything much that day.

That evening I sat in our living room with all the room lights off except for the Christmas tree. I remember looking at the Christmas tree, trying to find all the Christmas ornaments both boys made in school while growing up. It was always a tradition to hang all the ornaments they made as little boys in grade school. I was thinking about the night before at the jail. I had to get this all lined up in my head about Brady's court date, the court sentence, and how we get this family back together? I had no idea how to accomplish that feat. I felt like a blind man weaving in and out of traffic on the highway. Cars were honking and screaming at me to watch out, get out of the way, or you're going to get killed. That is precisely how I felt. My inner voice was screaming, watch out, get out of the way. You're going to get killed.

Chapter 3
It Is All on Me

I didn't realize it, but I had drifted into a long Christmas nap, reliving my past longing for an answer to make sense of this.

I realized I was re-thinking all my anger, shame, and hate for the past years and could not get a vision to resolve this mess. Funny, what I did best in the hospital was to quickly evaluate a problem or respond to a life-threatening crisis and make a plan because usually, a person's life depended on it. I just couldn't get my head wrapped around how to fix this one. I seem to be responding to all the family issues with anger and being impulsive, just like my dad. Everything I vowed I wasn't going to become - I was. I began to think that I had to make some significant changes in myself. How was that supposed to look, and how was that going to happen? The same thinking always seemed to come back to me.

I remember one late summer night, and there was a lot of yelling in front of our house. We were already in bed, and I looked out the windows only to see Kim's younger brother hollering at me from the yard of our two-story home: "Come out here. I am going to whip your ass." The truth of the matter is that Brady had seen his uncle that day and dumped all sorts of nonsense on him, and he believed him. Brady could convince anyone of anything because he has the gift of persuasion. I told Kim, "You better go down and deal with your dumb-ass brother, or I will take a baseball bat and knock him out." It wasn't about him, but the lie I believed her family felt about me that I was at fault for the whole Brady deal. My paranoid thoughts kept saying to me, "You rode all over Kim and your kids - she is just not saying what everyone is thinking: Dave, this is on you." I would think about how this whole thing started with me. Like most, I began to believe it. I had many flashbacks to my childhood. Surely, something got plugged into me wrong while I grew up with two brothers, Ron, the oldest, and Steve, the youngest.

Some outside noises awoke me from the Christmas nap.

I remember sitting there physically and emotionally wiped out from Christmas, work, and court. I do remember thinking back to my early childhood.

I have fond memories as a child growing up. It was unusual for a mother to work in the fifties and sixties. The norm for those days was to rely on the father to be the bread-winner. However, my mother was a self-starter and became one of the first women in Texas to be a credit manager for Sears Roebuck, one of the world's largest retail stores during that time. By standards of that era and today, people would consider my mom a successful professional working woman. My father worked for Humble Pipeline in the oil and gas business. Back then, West Texas was busy with new oil field discoveries in the Permian Basin, which is still one of the world's largest oil fields. My father worked in the office and seldom had to go out in the field. He had a technical role with piping systems. Both my parents had good jobs, and ours would be considered a financially successful family.

As both parents worked full time, it was not unusual to be left home with my older brother. During this time in our country's history, it was still uncommon for both parents to work. The wife was considered the homemaker and the one raising the kids. It was the days of a one-income family. I never thought much about it because it was customary for that time. I admit that I had thoughts about it because all my friends' mothers were at home. At my house, it was my big brother and me. I don't remember having any memories of feeling awkward or different from my friends. I took working hard for granted and that it was just part of my family's standards. It wasn't until I started studying fathering that I learned the decay of the family began in the era of both parents working full time. Kids became victims. As a silent epidemic, a thing called fatherlessness was taking shape. The impact of fathers and then mothers being away from home will later shape a catastrophic result for families, not only in the United States but in the world. Fatherlessness will become the Number One social epidemic of our time.

But for me, growing up in an oil-enriched town in West Texas came with fond memories. I can remember endless summer nights where the best childhood time of our lives was playing in the front yard. There were football games in the adjacent vacant lot and digging foxholes to play army with neighboring friends, usually from the next block. My big brother always included me in his activities. In retrospect, including me was his wisest choice because leaving me home meant risking me, "telling dad" that Ron went off without me. The fact of the matter, he rarely did that. I had looked up to my brother because he seemed to always care for me. We had the usual brother-to-brother hand combat and wrestling and him pulling pranks on me. In everything we did, I know he would always protect me and be on my side. I don't think he ever "sold me out" to mom and dad for messing up. But boy, did he threaten me on any given occasion for his advantage. Over time, I learned this trait from him. I knew how to turn it on him as we grew older.

It seemed Ron took the wrath of the first child growing up. I remember him often getting a belt whipping or yelled at by our dad too often. You would probably relate that to a bad kid, but my brother was the farthest thing from being bad. He was a typical kid growing up in a West Texas oil town where football and church ruled the town. I remember having respect for my brother, and later when he was in high school, I had respect and admiration because he took a load of crap from my dad. I didn't have words to describe what I saw between my dad and brother, but I knew to stay the "hell away" from dad when he was angry. Ron seemed to be the whipping post out of default.

In my memories, there suddenly appeared an image of my dad and brother. They were standing face to face with dares in their eyes. They had clenched fists. Who would hit first? Who was going to knock the shit out of the other? I remember running down the hallway to my room and making sure it was all clean and got in bed, thinking if he came down the hallway and saw me asleep that he would leave me alone.

With that, I Seemed to Jolt Out of My Drowsy Christmas Sleep.

Chapter 4
We Seemed Just Like Other Families

We seemed to be like many families growing up in the fifties with daily chores, including washing clothes, cleaning the house, and mowing the yard. There was the usual command from mom saying we could go outside only when we did our chores. We knew how to sweep, wash, and iron clothes, dust, plus clean and dry the dishes. Those were defining traits in my adult life that I found valuable in establishing my home. I can remember my mom saying if I wanted something ironed, then go iron it. She was very good at teaching us how to iron shirts and putting the right creases in the right places. I am still good at ironing to this date but probably not meeting the standard of my wife. And you would be correct in assuming all our clothes were from Sears Roebuck, where mom worked. I remember going to the store with my dad just before closing time to pick up my mom, and we could shop for clothes and get an employee discount. To this day, I rarely step in a Sears Roebuck store and have never purchased a piece of clothing. You see, most kids were wearing Levi's and not Roebucks. I was certainly not wearing the "in-crowd clothes." Mom always had a twist in telling us that we weren't like everyone else, and we should be grateful and thank the good Lord. Crap on that!

There was a ritual of going to pick up my mom from work at nine at night. I recall riding with my dad and sometimes my brother, and we would stop at the Southern Maid Donut shop and get hot donuts. That was the only donut shop growing up, and the cherry and chocolate donuts were heavenly. When I travel back to my hometown, I visit the same store in its original location and building. It is as if that same donut store remains frozen in time. Yes, you guessed it - the donuts didn't seem to be the same, although they looked just as I remember. Now, as I drive through my hometown, folks have died, buildings torn down, or barely standing. I realize each time I return that one of the most defining times of my life is quickly vanishing. I drive by my old schools, my boyhood neighborhoods, the church building, and our old family business service station. I often realize how important these years can be for little boys and girls and the importance of family, work, and church. I always tell men that I had a good childhood, but with all families, we had our secrets. I am not sure we would call them secrets during that time.

It was not unusual to get yelled at or get a belt across our butts. But later in life, with my brother, I saw more than belts. There was uncontrolled anger and temper from my dad. Today, I would call it rage. As I mentioned in my dream, I was the little brother. I knew when all hell broke out between my dad and brother to get out of sight, hoping my dad would not come down the hallway and get me. He rarely would, but I will never forget those encounters and mortal fear of his fist or open hand slap coming toward me. His words were more piercing than any blow he would give out. I can never remember getting a whippin' in grade school but later in junior high and high school.

There was this one Sunday night, and my dad had told me to take my little brother home from church because they were going to have a late board meeting. I remember driving up to our house late, and we had a gaslight in our front yard that came on at dusk. I got out of the car, and our house was pitch black. I had a bizarre and scary feeling about going in alone, and I didn't. I just knew that something did not feel right. My mom and dad drove up late, and my little brother, Steve, had fallen asleep in my lap underneath the gas lamp in the front yard. All hell and fury broke loose with my dad when he asked why Steve wasn't in bed. I told him I was too afraid to go into the house. I knew never to lie; knowing telling the truth got me no favors. The worst thing I could have ever done was to tell my dad that I was scared (of the dark), and he took me to every room in our house, turning on the lights, screaming at me that nothing was in there. He told me I was as bad as a little girl.

I got his uncontrolled fit of anger. He told me to go to my room, and he walked behind me and went to my closet. He got my favorite Davy Crockett belt I had kept since childhood. My belt was part of a childhood Christmas gift of toys about Davy Crockett because he was a legend in Texas during our revolution of independence from Mexico. I got trapped in our smaller bathroom with little space to maneuver on the floor, moving in circles with him just hitting me, telling me to stop moving. He kept yelling at me, asking me if I was ever going to do that again. In his rage of just hitting me blindly with the belt, the buckle slapped me across the face. I remembering lying to everyone at school the next day about why I had a black eye and whelp across my right eye from the metal buckle. The embarrassment and shame stuck with me for years. In today's world, parents would face an investigation for abuse to children.

I figured out the game really well and would do almost anything to keep from experiencing that again. Funny, I never remember my mother rushing to my aid and stopping my dad from whipping us. Never did I see my mom come to either my brother or my rescue from our dad. I always felt she manipulated my dad using his anger to "get us to behave." Gosh, we were the good kids on the block and were never the troublemakers. We were too afraid of getting caught. I think after my brother left home that I took his place. I had a different approach to my dad. I think it is safe to say I loved my dad but feared him. As noted in the Preface of this book by my younger son, Casey, you will read the same phrase. I know one thing; I made a vow not to be like my dad. In watching my dad die in his later years, I realized I had many good traits from him and a few I still guard very closely. I was glad to see my dad soften and become tender. However, a few outbursts would occasionally be there, usually out of frustration and impatience.

It seemed to be a standard in our home to play every school sport. So, I tried, but I never seemed good enough. It wasn't like I could participate in theater, band, or choir and not play a sport in our family. After all, life in West Texas was about football and winning. It was as if I didn't have a choice not to play a sport because my bigger brother, Ron, established the standard. He was good at everything he did, from running hurdles, basketball, baseball, and football. You see, it was an expectation of achievement. I can't remember the words, "just go out and have fun." That is what you did on the sandlot on Saturday with the neighbor kids. But when you played a school sport, it was all about winning. Ron was programed to be better than the next guy because my dad was insistent and dogmatic about winning. I don't remember hearing my dad say, "You played well, David. I am proud of you." It was always about what didn't happen that could have changed the game. My dad was the ultimate side-line critic whose rants followed in the car to home and many times into the next day. I was the little brother sitting next to my brother in the back seat with my dad spitting furor into the rearview mirror. By the way, that would be the same story of my two sons coming home from a soccer match sitting in the back seat of the car. The words would be very similar, if not exact.

Funny, I can remember only a few times of my dad playing with me or coaching me. Perhaps he saw that as something Ron should do, but we both knew that was not right. Ron was always sensitive to me being a part of what he did. When we went to the park to play football, and they divided into teams, yep, I was the last one chosen. But I got to be a part. That was big, and occasionally I would get a pass thrown to me. Somewhere I knew it was a "token" pass without any consequence if I dropped it or caught it. Hey, I got to be a part of my brother's life and those he grew up with at school and church. Looking back somehow, I think I had more identity with his friends than any of mine. I think being accepted as the little brother was more than just being David, the person. I don't remember thinking in those terms because I was a part of something. To this date, I keep up with some of his same friends.

I soon realized that sports would define a lot in my family's value system. The local football stadium was around the corner from our house, and we would walk to Friday night football games. I vividly remember going with my dad to games, and we would sit high in the stands to see all the field like a general looking at his battlefield. I heard him rant and rave at Ron to knock the hell out of them, get up-don't let them ever knock you down. You get them first. And on and on every game. I remember anticipating his behavior and would make a point to get away from him. It was there as a little boy I vowed never to be like my dad with my kids. I became exactly like my dad.

In that time and town, organized sports began in grade school. You had to try out for the team, and if you did not meet the standard, you simply did not play. You guessed it, I could not fail, and I had to make the team in every sport. Let me draw a picture of my brother and me. He was taller and bigger, and I was little and small. I didn't know that I would be the smallest male graduate of my high school. It also meant if I was to make the team that I would have to find ways to knock down bigger players my age because I was always the smallest player on the team. I dreaded the first day of practice because rarely did the pants and pads fit me, and the helmet looked like a big bowl on my head. You put them on and played. I ran like I was in some robot suit with little ability to move and be agile. There wasn't any going to the local shopping mall and buy special pads, pants, or helmets because they didn't look or feel just right.

Chapter 5
Sports, Church, Work, and Hormones

You get the picture – growing up in West Texas was about sports. It seemed if it wasn't about sports, school, and work, then it was about church. I remember vividly getting a haircut every Saturday during my lunch break while working for my dad. I would walk over to the barbershop on my lunch hour, take a number from a wooden stand by the door and pay my own seventy-five cents for a regular boy haircut. I was L.O.'s son. You see, L.O. had a flattop haircut and could pass as a welter-weight boxer and win every match. Everyone called my dad L.O. for Landis Oran, or they called him Clark.

As a kid, after a long day at a sandbox game or a game of army in the foxholes in the adjoining vacant lot, it was supper, baths, and getting everything ready for church. Later, as we grew, it was customary for us to work at the station every day. I remember scrubbing my skin off with Lava soap, thinking I would never have clean hands again from all the grease and oil penetrating every pore in my hands. I remember my dad's hands had deep cracks, and it seemed his blood in his hands was black. His hands were massive, tough skin, and when he made a fist, well, your imagination went wild. They were like iron fists.

I remember going home late after work on Saturdays, and he would always tell me to go in and get a bath and polish my shoes for church. It was not unusual to wear a bowtie and white shirt I ironed on Saturday night. I remember hating going to the bathtub because this evil bag with a hose and nozzle hung from the bath knobs. I remember it because my mother would give me this saltwater enema as a routine to keep me "cleaned out." Little did I know what she used it for and where that nozzle had been! I had no idea what a douche was for women. I just remember her calling me a greased pig sliding all over that tub and her demanding me to be still. Really? You want me just to sit there and have this 5-inch nozzle slammed up my ass and smile. I don't know what you would call that today, but it would not be pretty. I know I had to be the cleanest kid sitting in church the next day. I think to this day, none of the brothers have a hard time taking a crap.

My dad was a Sunday school teacher during most of my big brother's life, but I escaped him being my teacher. My brother was not quite so lucky. He would take his wrath non-stop, even at church. There sat dad teaching Sunday school class with my brother talking about Jesus when earlier in the week, he beat the crap out of him. You must be thinking as I am writing this: So, your dad was a Sunday School Teacher? Are you kidding me? Yep, he could put on that suit and tie and sit at the Lord's table and rip off prayers as good as anyone. Isn't that how it works? It seemed living with my dad, working with my dad, and then being in church every week was over the top. He was a deacon, elder, and board chairman throughout the 19 years I attended with my family in that same church. All that seemed relatively normal. It appeared that was life.

My dad directed a church building campaign that was very controversial for a new sanctuary and a building renovation. I thought church members would torch our house because so many folks were against it. It ended up being very controversial. I remember sneaking into late-night Sunday board meetings on the back row waiting to go home, and it was fiery and loud. It seemed families were drawing lines in the sand of how to pay for the new building. I remember our church was vibrant, and our best friends went to church, youth camps, and Sunday night youth programs. My life revolved around my folk's life in the church. We were faithful and loyal church members. By the way, the sanctuary got built along with renovations in the old church. Not because it was my dad, but he was dead right. Time would show it was the right decision for the church. I was always proud when I went back for a wedding or funeral and knew my dad made all that happen.

As I look back on life, the church was a great and positive experience and a foundational part of my life. I have very vivid memories in high school of being assigned to go with the church elders to the shut-in members at home or those in the hospital. It was a great excuse to get out of the church. The lessons of visiting the shut-in members made lasting impacts on my life. I learned more about ministering to people than any other experience in my life. I know God used those experiences to imprint on me a love for the "unfortunate, sick, and dying." I don't remember saying much riding in the car with the "church elders," but all of them knew my dad, and I had to be on best behavior. I was taught early respect at home even though I could never point you to those discussions or "round table talks at dinner time." I don't think we ever prayed but at Sunday lunch. In later years when my family would have a meal with my folks that I had to remind my parents to pray before any meal or occasion with grandchildren.

I think I remember this time of my life as one of the best times because of families' fellowship. There were weekends filled with church friends playing card games like canasta and always taking pies and covered dishes on Saturday nights and Sunday night church programs. It always seemed more formal, with my mom wearing a dress, and my dad always wore a nice casual shirt, shined shoes, and pleated slacks. I never saw my dad wear jeans. In looking back, they always dressed for the occasion. I guess no one could make Sears Roebuck's clothes look better than my mom's. I think the only other significant store to buy clothes in town was J.C. Penney. I remember that manners were important. At that time, we learned table manners, greeting people, and courtesy in grade school. You learned to set the table and always sit a young woman first. Everyone waited until all female guests sat in their chairs before you could sit. And, of course, you opened doors for females. It was always very disciplined and important. I learned the importance of greeting people by their last names, shaking a man's hand firmly, and being polite to females as foundational behavior. Of course, mom and dad strengthened those lessons at home as they occurred. I learned to dance and stand in the corner of a large auditorium, vowing not to ask a girl to dance in formal dance cotillions or called a dance club today. I eventually stepped out there when the adult sponsors were literally throwing us out in the middle of the dance floor. I might have fallen in love a dozen times during that time but too embarrassed to ever admit it. Remember, I said I was always the smallest kid in class, even my senior year of high school. That meant I still had to dance with taller girls. You know, girls hit puberty first, and they get taller and grow breasts. That became an advantage at the dance nights. I would fantasize about putting my head on their breasts. Of course, you kept two feet distance from each other dancing.

Naturally, you always took your best friend whom you could trust to your death – or so the vow went in the infamous treehouse that all you and your friends built in a big tree in the backyard for a clubhouse. I remember the show in America called The Little Rascals was famous. They made making a clubhouse cool. What was even better was to get airborne in a tree. Amazingly, we did not fall out of a tree with simple nails holding wood together in the tree limbs. We had members, but only our best friends got voted into the club. No kid that wasn't cool ever played with us and no girls could enter our territory! Our secrets were sacred.

I have a vivid memory of the girl who lived down the street from us. I guess I was ten or eleven, but I remember a family down the street with two girls around the ages of my brother and me. They lived in a better house because it was not like our wood-frame house with shingles. It seemed huge with a big tall concrete fence. It seemed obvious even to us that they had more money. My brother sort of had a thing for the older sister. All that made it easy for us to go with our parents on card night. I think that was the kick-off of being curious about sex and my hormones. The little sister was a little ahead of her time if I remember. Of course, I did. She had breasts. And there was more, she rounded out toward the bottom, and I knew this was a pretty big deal. At eleven or twelve, you begin to add some things up, mostly if you listen to your big brother's friends. If they talked about breasts and asses, then by golly, I should too.

I remember thinking about how I could get this female anatomy figured out because my brother's friends talked a lot about sex. I remember paying her twenty-five cents for her to pull her panties down. For the life of me, I had no idea what I was looking at, and it made no sense to me. All I know, there was a slit with no penis. I was sort of confused and pondered over that for some time to come. You see, I thought much later that she never asked to look at my penis. I am thankful for this very day because what I didn't realize at that time that I probably didn't stack up like other boys my age. Of course, I could not ask anyone about what I saw because I was supposed to know. My mother did clear that up a little later in life. Of course, the word got out that my mom had to clue me on the anatomy. I think my dad was relieved. We never talked about it again. I lost track of the neighbor girl when they moved, but I never forgot her. It was my first encounter with SEX. My dad never talked to me about sex or anything remotely about sex, but he gave me a book with pictures that made absolutely no sense to me. However, it didn't replace the Sears Roebuck catalog Lingerie section. That was sex education in the fifties.

My mother grew up in the country with four sisters and no brothers. She would tell us about when they worked all day, and they would clean up and put on what we might call nighties or nightgowns. Well, when my mom came home from work, she would shag the clothes just like when she grew up. I remember it was routine when I was in grade school that I would be in the bathtub or taking a dump that my mom would just walk into the bathroom and began to put on her makeup. I will never forget her waving hair spray all over the bathroom and suffocating me. I will always remember Aqua Net Hairspray to this day. Conservatively speaking, my mom was naked half the time. So, I had no misunderstanding of what breasts looked like, but my mom's breasts were monsters. I would imagine you would think that is how all breasts would look at my age. To this day, as my mom aged and other people, including great-granddaughters, would help her get dressed, they would come out of her bedroom with this shocked look with just a funny smile. It was like they could not get words out. We would all just look at them smiling, not saying anything because they saw mamma's tits. I guess you would say that I got sex education by osmosis.

Chapter 6
Can I Fill it up with Regular or Premium Gas?

The Day after Christmas.

The day after Christmas, for most people, was a part of the holiday vacation. Why would I think the day was any different when, growing up, we only closed our gas station on Christmas Day? I remember being on administrative call at the hospital. That meant going up for the day to make rounds, visit patients, and talk to doctors. It was just another day at work. After all, hospitals don't sleep or slow down with sick patients and surgeries.

On the way to the hospital, I remember stopping for gas at a local drive-up grocery and gas station. I got out and threw the gas handle in the car, reminiscing that I would meet cars driving up in our service station and asking them, Regular or Premium? Then, can we check those tires or oil and sweep out your floorboard? I remember sitting there looking through my dirty windshield, hoping my oil and tires were OK. The floorboard was, for sure messy.

I started thinking about what changes have come from full-service stations with gas at 0.20 cents per gallon to $2.50 per gallon. Now I pump my own gas and drive off with a dirty windshield and forget about your floorboard vacuumed. I think I snarled a bit, thinking of how it was.

Things started to change in our home with my dad's career with Humble Pipeline. There was an opportunity to own a Humble Service Station on the opposite side of the town – Eastside. Today, these stations are referred to as Exxon. We lived on the Westside or considered the original town with old money and older homes with families of multiple generations. And we were moving to the new side of town with a new high school. We would be on the edge of town with few homes. Is dad crazy? What the heck did we know about fixing flats, gasoline, oil changes, and running a business? We learned fast. Shortly we had the biggest and busiest Humble service station in all West Texas. We worked our butts off day and night. We all worked.

My dad went from being physically out of shape to a Mr. Atlas. That was the name of the product line for tires, oil, and car accessories. My God, he could barely bend his arm without busting out his shirt sleeves. His station became the model of "5-Star" full services. Our station won numerous awards for growth, customer satisfaction, and being a model of the new service station design with two over-head canopies, three service bays, green shopping stamps, and home car customer delivery. Yes, we would not only get your car and clean it but deliver it back home. It is with this experience a lot of things started to happen in our family.

My dad was obsessed that everything had to be immaculately clean. Our station concrete driveway was cleaned with a special solvent, mopped (yes, mopped), hosed down with soap and water, and then squeegeed off. Everything that required paint had regular paint jobs. Somebody cleaned every oil can daily. Our service station was cleaner than any home in town. To say you could eat lunch on the driveway of our gas station was an understatement. During this time, we hired porters to work in the work bays washing and changing the oil and fixing flats. It is here that I learned about cars, changing spark plugs, detailing vehicles by hand waxing to get that brand-new car appearance. There was no such thing as an electric car paint buffer.

My dad would walk around cars with his cigar in his mouth, inspecting windows for streaks or missed spots, and you would do them again and again. We were about perfection. It was like a sports game. We executed with a plan, a coach, an owner, a dad, and a drill sergeant wrapped up in one person with a Roy Tan cigar in his mouth. Don't get me wrong. My dad worked harder than anybody. You may have been the boss's son, but you would work harder and longer than anyone. At 13 years old, I could run the station and manage anything like my dad. When my brother graduated, married, and left town, I could do it all. We wore official Humble uniforms with a baseball hat, red leather belts, grey uniforms, and work boots. I remember summer was a dreaded time because you woke up at five am, got dressed, and ate a full sit-down breakfast with eggs, bacon, and biscuits – every day. I would ride to work with my dad in the old truck, and I would open the station up for business while he counted the money and did inventory. We did inventory every day. My dad knew every day how many tires or cans of oil we sold every day.

We had our routine daily drive across town to work until we moved to the East side of town. In most cases, I would walk to work. I remembered only one family vacation my entire childhood. It was to the Colorado mountains in a cabin next to a lake where we used a rowboat. Sixty years later, I could take you to the exact location we stayed for a few days. On special holidays, we would load up in our car and drive all night to a grandparent's home for a holiday. It was always a night drive because cars did not have air conditioners. We had to work a full day before leaving. I always got the hot floorboard while my bigger brother got the seat. I think I can remember each trip to this day because it was the only time we would travel as a family. These were fond memories and perhaps the most pleasant of my youth. The trips were always fun, with mom baking cookies and making spam and tuna fish sandwiches. The time with all the relatives was a highlight and one of my most fond memories. They remain etched in my memories.

I got a clear picture of family members sitting at the table playing dominoes or going to the downtown barbershop with my granddad. One granddad was a truck farmer in East Texas, and one was the town barber in West Texas. I learned from one granddad to feed poor people or give the shirt off your back if you needed to help someone (which he did). The other granddad was a professional barber that every man and woman in town knew by name. In those days, the beauty shop and barbershop were in the same building as Archie. Archie was the shoeshine man who was an elderly black man who was like family. I never thought of him as any different than me. To this day, I have Archie's shoeshine stool in my office, where he sat, giving hundreds of shoeshines.

I saw that granddad making sure Archie and his family had enough food, clothes, and shoes. My other granddad was a truck farmer, and he would make sure no black person would go hungry in his town. Obviously, he knew others felt different but regardless of color or anything, they cared for people. Both of my granddads were enormous advocates for black people in every respect of life and living. To both, the color was no factor. That trait transferred to my generation from my two granddads. My dad daily demonstrated to take care of people who had little themselves. You never got a hand-out, but you worked for your dignity and self-worth. It became about teaching responsibility and personal worth. I later learned the life lesson word was "injustice," which became a trademark of my family to fight against.

Most of all, my junior high and high school years were at the service station. I later struggled with the job because the East side of town became the rich side of town, and our station served many rich people. I guess my self-image of what my family did for a living touched me deeply. We were the service station family who put gas in cars and cleaned them up – mainly for the rich folks. Many of my friends at school drove cool cars. It seemed there was always a school cheerleader or majorette in the car of a football player on Friday or Saturday nights for a date. Those were still my nights to work and close the station at ten o'clock. I seldom viewed the station as "the best in West Texas," as I found myself putting a dollar of gas in fellow students' cars on a Friday night date. In some way, I felt I was the "boy" cleaning the window and pumping the gas for rich white folks. Ironically, the black men who worked with me sensed that and would always tell me I would be better for it because I knew how to work for a dollar. I am not sure that ever felt OK for them or me in life. They were right. I remember them today because they were family. I clearly understood growing up in the sixties with school segregation, the "N" word, and how race tore up every stitch of friendship, family, community, and country. I owe my sense of right, wrong, ethics, race, work, equality, faith, and such to the males of my family. Both my sons have a strong sense of these values, for which I am grateful they watched and listened.

Chapter 7
Life Took a Major Turn

Things began to change for my family. My older brother could finish high school on the Westside of town and not attend the new high school in his senior year. My little brother, Steve, was born and was beginning to be more of an observer during this time. Ron was about out of high school when Steve started growing up. We all had about six to eight years between us. Steve barely knew Ron before he graduated from high school and left town. During this time, my brother and dad seemed to be having "knockdown fights in the den of our house." My dad looked like a prizefighter. My brother was an all-district linebacker and tight end in football. If one said the stop sign was red, the other would say it was green. I am not sure how all that worked because I was six years younger than my brother. I just know that the family dynamics changed in our house. It was full of anger and disappointment. My brother was dating a pretty girl in high school and later married. They had a little girl the next year. He got her pregnant out of wedlock. Wow, there was talk at that time of nuclear warheads in Cuba during the Cuban Missile Crisis, but I saw the real thing in my house. Of all things, my brother's senior year was a mess. He was married to a girl who was a junior in high school. That time in our family became a defining time in acceptance, rejection, disbelief, and my dad, the church elder, would be a grandfather. Somewhere this was not in the plan.

I think I just found ways to disappear during that time. The conflict was toxic. It seemed like a bad dream, at the same time, a big blur. All I know is that I saw my first clear look at rejection, conditional love, and anger that lasted for years. The good news is that everyone loved his girlfriend and soon-to-be his wife. He got married, and our family took off in an unexpected direction. I loved her as she was like a sister to me, and she drove a little red convertible car. I went with her everywhere. As a young kid, I realized she could be like someone I want to marry.

I think maybe I got left behind somewhere in all the discourse in life. I realized things with sports and school and friends were taking a turn. I witnessed my family change in ways with what little laughter and joy evaporated. I can never remember talking about this crisis as a family, praying for our family, and healing. These were only foreign words for us as "church people." I can say I never heard those teachings in my church or family. I never remember family teachings, fathering, discipleship, marriage, and the list continues. I realized my family worked and grew up in the depression and walking to school in the snow with cardboard in their shoes. It was a fact, but I was sick of hearing it. It was like a badge of courage for our family. At that time in my life, it seemed like a chain around my neck.

As I said, I was small in stature. Of all things in my life, I did not "make the cut" to move on to play high school football. After five years of starting on grade school and junior high football teams playing defense and offense, I was out. Even though I was the smallest kid on the field, I was always on the first team. I was a real hustler, and my big brother had taught me to go low to knock down bigger players, and I mastered that technique. Somehow the voices went off in my head from my dad telling my brother to take them out, knock them down and win.

The ritual for trying out for the high school football team happened the year before you would go to high school. You had to pad up and be on the field. The high school coaches would come to our school in practice to choose who would play high school football. You had to line up in a straight line like prisoners in a line-up. The high school coaches would walk by you to decide if you would even have a chance at playing high school football. The high school coach not only walked by me but came back and gave me this pathetic look.

He told me I should play tennis or something. If I knew I would not get killed at home by my dad, I would have used every curse word I ever heard of years in a service station to that coach. By the way, he was right.

I was too small to play high school football. That rejection would prove to be a motivator and a point of sacrifice that stayed with me for many years in my adult life. At that time, I began having trouble in school with math, and I struggled with memorization. My folks paid for a tutor, and that was an extreme luxury with our home budget. I would pass. It might have something to do that the tutor was a female high school senior that had, yes, great breasts! I loved doing math. I had a huge crush on her. She must have shaken her head and laughed every time I went home after class.

For the life of me, I could not memorize the simplest of poems, and math was a nightmare. It was the first release of this foreign math called Algebra. Good, God! What the hell was that? Then there was Geometry. I could even care less about fractions and formulas. Who the hell thought this crap was going to help us with anything? I avoided anything that looked like this type of math, even through college. It might as well be Chinese.

Well, I had to play sports, but what? It wasn't a part of the picture for me to be in choir, band, or not play sports in our family. That coach I hated for a very long time who told me to play tennis or something? Imagine this, I played tennis in high school and junior college, and I did well. I was a powerful force with fast serves and hard groundstrokes. I lettered and got the same letter jacket as the football players but with a tennis racket on the school emblem. I knew somewhere my dad thought I was a failure in not making it in a real sport. I played tennis by myself using a backboard until I couldn't see the ball at night. I didn't have anyone I could play with, and so it was Mr. Green Backboard at the high school tennis courts. I was the kid at the end of the court's pounding balls until I couldn't see them at night. Then I would save my money and buy balls with a fluorescent covering that you could see better at night.

I had great groundstrokes, and the backboard became my contender. I never felt great about playing with someone for a long time because I only knew what I saw or read about tennis. I never went to a tennis camp or got special training. I learned mostly from myself. I never had a good self-image about my abilities. I had played all the other sports but never this tennis game. I never had a new racket because my dad would never purchase one, much less balls to practice. I would use a hand-me-down tennis racket from a guy who befriended me in helping me with the game. To this day, we are still friends. He had no reason to be my friend as he was a year younger and a terrific player. During the summers between school years, he went to all the tournaments and tennis camps. He never worked in high school as his dad had a profitable accounting business. Me? I worked. Despite that, we remained good friends.

My dad never watched me practice nor ever attended a tennis match. Never. I think that was worse than any whipping or slurred comment to me or any "go to hell" failure look. I remember our family had a brown Bel Aire Chevrolet we bought one vacation visiting our grandparents in East Texas. At every local match, I looked for that car, hoping my dad would drive up to watch me play. My dad took me to every track meet, baseball game, or football game to watch my brother. Yet my dad never watched me play one match. There was only an idle conversation at the supper table at night without him raising his head in acknowledgment. I was pretty good. Do you sense some rejection, anger, disappointment, failure, and image issues? You bet. Later in life, in personal counseling, I had the challenge and ultimate realization that "little Dave" was hurt. There was a disconnect between Dave, the man, father, husband, and Dave, the little boy. That proved to be a painful journey to become one with myself later in my life. As that little boy, I just knew he hurt a lot, and there was no one to rescue him. I later discovered this hurt or fracture would cause me bitter issues in my family, work, and relationships.

In my world, I was just Ok. I found three or four friends in high school, and I struggled with high school because of my size. I realized I was the Sears Roebuck guy in a world of Levi jeans, madras shirts, and penny loafers. My self-image was fragile. Today, I wear Levi's, madras shirts, and wear the original shoe design of penny loafers. That seems funny now as I like the look. It is not just about wearing the clothes I never had or could afford. I liked them and never could put my hand on them till much later in life. For many, when you finally get what you always wanted, it was not that big of a deal. For me, that was not true. Maybe I am a 72-year-old prep?

Life Took a Major Turn

Life in West Texas had its moments. During the summer, we got to attend the summer church camps joining other similar denominational church groups in West Texas. The one thing I could count on is that I would fall in love with a girl from another town while at camp. I liked girls, and I hoped they liked me, but I could never get in my head that I was worthy enough. The one thing going for me was we moved into a brand-new brick house. Our furniture was nice because my dad would trade-out dental work and furniture from two customers who did business with our station. I had a high voice as I later found out as an adult that my pituitary gland was only half the average size. That meant that I grew up with a poorly performing male hormone. We never thought about medical terms during those times. You rarely went to the doctor and never to the hospital. Who would have guessed? I guess having blonde hair, short stature, well-tanned from tennis and work, and "dimples" kept me in the race. Everyone loved my dimples, which tended to embarrass me more than anything else.

The girls I liked were of similar neighborhood and income, with one exception. That exception was a big one because my mixed doubles partner on the varsity tennis team was "Miss Permian High School." She was on the elite peppette or cheer squad and every committee in the school. She was pretty, very popular, and friendly. Her brother was an all-state tennis player who let me play with him as a sophomore. He was a senior.

She asked Me to escort her to the senior homecoming. I was "her friend." We were about the same height, and it was cool. It blew a lot of folks' minds because I was not one of the in-crowd guys. In those days, schools had fraternity and sorority clubs like universities. You guessed it. I wouldn't even take the chance of being rejected in a club. They were truly the "in-thing" at high school because you wore emblem jackets and sweaters just like the show American Pie. To see me in the middle of the football field and later at the Homecoming dance, I hit the top. Guess what?

Life went back to normal Monday following Homecoming weekend. I thought of her a lot after high school graduation, but I knew she was a girl out of my league. I could accept that reality because she was in places and events I would never fit without the money or prestige. Over time, she faded away from any possibility as she went to Texas Christian University (TCU), where my brother earlier attended. I went to the local junior college in town. I think I had a fantasy of living in her world. Still, she lived fast with family money, college plans, and popularity. I think she liked me because I was somebody who liked her for just being her. I could be just a guy whose folks ran the gas station. I think the many hours on the tennis court and traveling to tournaments must have represented some things she wanted in a guy but never found. I never saw her again after high school until I attended a fifty-year class school reunion. It was there I realized I did have the most beautiful wife at the event. Sadly, age and crippling disease made her look older and less attractive. I came to the reality I liked her a lot in high school. I probably liked her a whole lot. It was like falling in love with Cinderella and watching her being escorted to the ball by the handsome knight and me going home with the reality of who I was. I was a middle-class working kid whose family worked for everything they got in life. I was angry, disappointed, rejected, and never felt worthy or good enough.

Somehow, my mom drilled into us a thousand times that we should be grateful for everything in life we have, and we needed to be respectful of it. No, mom, I was angry, not knowing how to direct my disappointments because we didn't talk and share things like many families. I don't remember experiencing our family sitting together sharing activities of our lives. I realized I yearned for intimacy. I realized seeing little of it demonstrated or discussed because I grew up in a task-oriented work environment. It sounds like I am still mad, but years of self-reflection, personal counseling, and a transformative spiritual experience allowed me to experience deep healing. Oddly I think my mom drove herself to be a self-made professional woman proving to the world she had value and importance. She was done being the farm girl.

I think I only got one award at school, and it was significant and a shock. We had school dances one Friday a month. I was encouraged to attend one Friday, and to my surprise, students chose me as the favorite at the dance based on a popular vote. It was a western dance, and I was named Mr. Howdy. It made me realize that more people liked me than I thought. To this date, I can hear the clapping and hooting, and I could walk you to that same room today. Outside of lettering in tennis and the Number 2 seed on the varsity tennis team, that was about it for high school. The Number 1 seed was the kid who was a year behind me who gave me his used tennis rackets, and somewhere I guess he needed a friend as much as me.

I was only average in classes but never a troublemaker. Are you kidding? It meant if I got in trouble at school and got a "swat," I got more than a swat from dad when I got home. I knew my dad would defend me if necessary, but heaven help me if I was the problem. On one defining occasion, I knew my dad "really defended me" in a math class. A guy sitting behind me in math class tried to look over my shoulder and cheat on a test. I mean, how funny is that or desperate this other guy would get answers from my test. The kid who had a tutor just to pass.

I remember the incident vividly. I found myself in the office with the Dean of Men for talking during that test. I was guilty. I told the guy sitting behind me to quit looking at my test paper. I was afraid the teacher would think I was cheating. My dad had always taught me that if there was an injustice to never hesitate in calling him for help. There is that injustice deal again. Well, the Dean of Men was an ex-Marine who looked like a tank commando. He had a flattop haircut like my dad and was short and stout. The Dean branded me guilty and took me to the middle of the main hallway in school. He told me to bend down and get three butt swats. He had a reputation for lifting guys off the floor when he gave them swats. Today, that man would probably go to jail for the cruelty of kids. He would leave whelps on guys butts. Well, I told him "No" and to call my dad. You guessed it; he traded at our service station. He knew my dad well.

My dad had been in the Army Air Corps in WWII and was in better shape than even the ex-tank commando, the Dean of Men. So, my dad enters the school office in his Humble uniform. I was terrified that I might have made the wrong decision. My dad walked directly to me without talking to anyone and said, "What happened"? I told him, and he asked me if I was lying. I mean, seriously, I watched him for two years trying to beat the hell out of my older brother. I said No, and he went over to the Dean of Men, who had a three-foot-stained flat and thinly cut butt splatter board with holes in it and swung it like a baseball bat. He said to him, "Jack (the Dean), if you want to give my kid a lick, you give it to me first, and then I will give you the next lick because my son says this is all wrong." How vivid is that moment over fifty years later that my dad defended me? We never talked about it again.

We lost a customer over that incident, and my dad never looked back. If you were right, you got defended. I can remember countless customers that accused one of our porters of some crazy thing because they were just black. My dad would walk out to their car and politely say to them never to drive into our station again. If you were wrong, you got a talk in the back-service bay or maybe lost part of your pay for the day or told to go home and not return. My dad knew color was an issue with white people thinking they must be bad people. Even after segregation, things didn't change as our government had planned. It was odd that our family moved to the "rich part of town," and a new grade school was built two blocks from our house. I walked to school every day.

What was terrible about the controversy about blacks bused to other schools is that they were bused across town with a school down the block from their house. With all the issues with segregation and integration with black kids was that I got bused. So, every day, my sixth-grade class had to be bused across town for racial equality. I didn't like it, but I just accepted it and went on with life. One thing I knew about our family is that we would have constructed a brick wall around our station, defending the black men working for us. It offended us to the core of our beliefs and values of how whites treated blacks. One of their sisters worked for us at our home, virtually raising my little brother. Her name was the same as my mother – Laverne. Never one time did we ever call or think of her as a maid. She was just Laverne. Over sixty years later, we still make contact with her and visit her.

After high school, my big brother decided to be in the ministry and go to Texas Christian University in Fort Worth, Texas. For the life of me, I couldn't even figure that out, except church was a positive factor in our lives. Well, it strained the very financial and physical limitations of our family. We drove many miles, taking clothes, food, and some money to my brother many weekends to help them manage. He worked odd jobs and graduated from TCU. He readily was accepted to Brite Divinity School or seminary. He accomplished what I knew; only a very few could do. I don't know for a fact, but I never heard my dad complement my brother or brag about him.

If he did, he never demonstrated that to me as a life lesson. I knew my brother did what few could have done, and he did it well. I will never know all that my brother had to do to cope with his decisions. I know they were monstrous.

My senior year in high school was a year just to get done. I remember taking our senior class picture, and the smart-ass photographer hollered at me, "hey, you short guy, come down on the front row and sit here in the middle." If I could have shot up "the middle finger" and still graduated, he would have not only got that but the spoken words associated with the middle finger. Smart Ass! Yep, I was the shortest guy in my senior class. I graduated and was glad. I ended up getting a church scholarship to the local junior college and continued to work for my dad. I had in my mind I could be a church youth director. As I said, the church was a positive factor.

Little did I know through all my youth and one-fourth of my marriage, I had a significant defect in my pituitary gland in my brain. This whole issue with my pituitary gland was my lack of growth and maturity all through school and my early marriage. It would also be a significant factor in fighting erratic emotional behavior. That made a lot of sense. I remember going into the hospital where I worked to get a CT Scan in the radiology department. They used this dye to "light up my brain" …funny. See, dad, "I had a brain!" But five minutes into the dye infusion, I had a major allergic reaction, and my airway started closing. I had swollen up like a pig. The whole CT scan team panicked and infused Benadryl too fast and blew my IV in my arm. Hell, I laid there thinking I am the Director of the Respiratory Therapy Department, and I will suffocate in the damn radiology CT scan room. Fortunately, a doctor ran in and got a new IV. It showed my pituitary gland was half the size of a normal gland. I had never been producing enough hormones, including male testosterone, after puberty.

I remember going back to the doctor's office, and he said, "Bend down and let me give you 1cc of testosterone and see how you feel and call me the next day. Good, God! I walked around like a Viagra commercial with a new feeling and bulge. Just like that, I felt I was on a big high. Is this what normal felt? It changed my entire life, and I think Kim got part of her answer for living with a husband with erratic behavior and erratic mood swings. At least I had a part of the answer that I wasn't just a butthole.

As you are reading, I hope you're not getting caught up, just in the gritty details in my childhood stories. I am hoping as we go, maybe you can correlate some of my life stories to some of yours. Hopefully, it brings back into memory some things that have proven obstacles for you as a father. Talking about our stories and hearing other men's stories is important. I think remembering the memories we unconsciously tucked away are important for us to confront. You may hear some common threads of anger, disappointment, and issues about our family legacies and our responses. I am really not a big reader except out of necessity with a professional work journal. When I picked up a book like this, I looked for what I have in common with the writer. It is my goal that my story is working itself into some conclusions about your fatherhood journey. I hope you are beginning to see how your entire fathering formation began as a little boy, not as a man who got married and had a kid. My story is not just about how some things happened in my family. It is meant to take you back in your memories of being a son, a child, a teen, a family member, and off to college and marriage. Keep traveling with me because all these issues (and more) become obstacles to us in being effective fathers. It will lead us to the Seven Secrets.

Chapter 8
Leaving and Starting on My Terms

I came home late that night from being on call at the hospital and just slipped into bed.

The good thing about Kim is usually when her head hits the pillow; it usually means she is sound asleep. I remember her awakening early the next morning. I just decided to lay there and found myself in and out of multiple dreams. Kim came upstairs to check on me and asked me if I was Ok. I said I felt I had been on a bad ride with bad dreams mixed in with good ones. I felt exhausted. She said she would fix some coffee, and why don't I come down and drink a cup with her.

I told her I had been thinking about the prior Christmas. Brady was living with some girl with another guy's baby. My total fear was he would get her pregnant. That picture was not going to be the treasured family we had prayed for in years past. Crap. What a disaster. It seemed like living another nightmare as it was familiar with my brother. We were excited that Brady was coming home for Christmas. That was a big deal because he rarely came home. We had all the house locks changed, so Brady could not come in and steal from us for drug money or whatever we had in our mind of what he was doing.

Since he either stole or traded anything of value for money, Christmas was about a coat, gloves, or something warm. Kim had been in the kitchen all morning cooking everything Brady liked for

Christmas. Brady was all about tradition. The house was perfect, and there was hope that things were turning in some positive way. Casey and I were in the front yard, and he drove up with this kid and girl. I thought this would be easy for me as I said hello, and out came the girl and kid. I remember it well, saying, "Brady, we love you and welcome you, but the girl and kid could not join us for Christmas." Yep, I threw out the biggest flame a human could throw, and he said, "fine, I am out of here." I was stunned he made that choice, but afterward, in reliving the moment, it was easy to figure out that anything I would say or throw out, he would send it back my way. I needed to let him know that of all the things hurling down the drainpipe was going to stop at this one. We weren't going to grandkid another man's son and some punked-out girl. Merry Christmas. Not going to happen.

Not even thinking, I looked into the house. Kim was at the sink finishing up dinner, and I had to walk in and tell her what happened. I walked up to the kitchen sink and told her Brady had come, and before I could get it out, she was hurrying to the window only to see him driving off. I begin telling her the story, and all she heard was that I got into it again with Brady. She went upstairs and just cried. Casey went to his room, and that was Christmas at the Clarks.

I had gone outside to mess with the car. I walked into the house, and Kim was upstairs, lying on the bed. Suddenly, we found ourselves lying on the bed in silence, and I caught myself looking back at things. I remember thinking about quitting my job, but I had no way to make an income. Funny, it made me think back to my dad. It must have been about the same age when my dad experienced a mid-life crisis leaving our successful service station business. During that time, my mother quit Sears Roebuck. Darn, no more Roebuck jeans. She ended up operating a Nursing home, and my dad probably found his true calling. He went to school at night, passed the first Texas nursing home license board, and graduated from the first class.

Imagine that. The Clarks went from pumping gas and fixing flats to changing bedpans and cleaning pee and waste out of beds. There we were, feeding people drooling in their wheelchair and watching the Soaps on TV in the Day Room. Yep, crazy. I became the backup cook, dishwasher, floor buffer, commode plunger expert, and god knows what else. My qualifications were top of the list from working at the station. It was during this time I learned a lot about taking care of older people. It was here I learned from my parents to love and care for older people and being sensitive to their needs. I remember waxing and buffing the long hallways at night while they slept and hearing some moan, cry and scream. I learned the high value of caring for older people and being passionate about their feelings and needs. To this day, both sons have high respect and passion for listening, caring, and loving older people. They will intently listen to every word an older person will say. They understand the importance of paying attention to folks whose days may go without ever seeing a grandchild or family member.

As I lay there, I remember thinking back to the last days at home with my parents, thinking I was so ready to move on with my life. Ironically, I was having the same thoughts. I was so prepared then to move on with life. Here I laid, thinking I was so ready to get the Brady thing behind us and move on.

In junior college, I knew going to college at TCU was out because of the cost. I was not going to a school my brother went to, so I turned West and wound up at the University of Texas at El Paso. I am the one who went to a town called hell, but it sure beats being drafted to a major conflict called the Viet Nam war.

The war was going on. If you stayed in school, you got an educational deferment or exclusion not to enter the army. It meant you could continue with your education. I had no earthly idea of what to do in life, but I knew people had to be part of the formula. In college, I was a psychology major and minor in Social Work. I flew past classes in Junior College and played tennis. For some reason, something got better in my head. But the Ninth Wonder of the World was at my fingertips – Juarez, Mexico. Oh my! I could drink, smoke, and go to strip bars, which I attended better than any church. As paranoid as I was about being taught right and wrong, I always looked for my dad to walk in the strip joint door. I knew it violated everything I was taught all my life, especially respecting women and drinking and smoking. However, I jumped over that hurdle with glazing speed.

Ron would have been amazed at how fast and high I jumped that hurdle. I gave guided tours to friends who came to the Army Boot camp at Fort Bliss, Texas, waiting on their deployment to the Viet Nam War as if I was a regular to strip joints or whore houses. The fact of the matter, I never gave up my virginity to the day I walked down the church aisle. I have to admit it was so crucial for me to "fit in and be a regular guy." I permitted myself to lie about being the experienced Juarez tour guy to strip joints and bars. I was totally aware I was breaking another family standard drilled into my head. I realized I lied about who I was as a man and sacrificed a deep value for being someone other than me. I have regretted that to this day. It later became a personal foundational character trait of always be who you are and be proud of it and never change for what others want you to be.

I talked and bragged as though I was the foremost gigolo in Mexico. There would be no question from my nighttime lying that I knew the clubs, the women by name, and every street in town. We did a lot of drinking and smuggling liquor in the floor toolbox of my Volkswagen Beatle across the border. There was a customs limit, and we exceeded it each trip. I must admit we were frequent fliers in Mexico. It became a big reason that I flunked out of college.

I remember one-night drinking so much that I didn't know how I got home. I just remember waking up in the bathtub next to the toilet because I was vomiting so bad. I later learned I had the dry heaves from vomiting up my toenails. My roommate got worried, and since he worked at the hospital, he knew nurses who could smuggle out IV bags. I had one hanging from the showerhead in the bathtub, where I fixed a bed next to the toilet. Today, we would probably call that "alcohol poisoning," It took me three days to recover. I could never smell bourbon again to this day. That was the end of drinking hard liquor. I had to persuade my roommate not to call my dad about my condition because I knew he would go ahead and kill me. He had already made one trip to El Paso, and it was for an even worse issue.

The Viet Nam war was in progress, and there were a bunch of kids that were going to stage a protest on a Sunday night in a busy street by the university. My roommate and I were guys from West Texas, and we said, "Let's go!" We were not against the war but thought it was cool. It was cool until the next morning at 8:00 a.m., and the door to our apartment had a knock. It was my dad! He had his Humble uniform on, and how he found our apartment is still a mystery. He or my mom never came to El Paso to visit me. I was shocked to hear his name, "Mr. Clark, come on in!" My roommate knew my dad and was naïve enough to think something terrible was going on. I was in my bedroom and heard the conversation.

I shot out of bed like a rocket going to the moon. My roommate invited my dad into the apartment, and he refused, of course. I remember him asking me one question at the front door: "Was that you that I saw on the national 10 pm news last night." I was clueless. Before I could explain to him, we were just messing around and had no intent to be against the war, and he said, "No son of mine will ever protest a war." He turned around and walked off and drove home. Well, home was 8 hours down the highway! He had to have got up from the television that Sunday night, got dressed, and drove straight to El Paso, Texas. I think it was one of those fathering times that he knew I was telling him the truth (and I was just stupid), but he drove off. He never said another word to me about it, even to his last day of life.

Although I could say in my head at the end of the day, "I will find my way home to my upbringing and be a better guy over it." Big lie. The fact of the matter is that I flunked out of the University of Texas at El Paso and had to go back home to the same junior college to stay out of the Viet Nam war. I lived by myself most of my time in college, and I was lonely, lost, depressed, and had no clue where life was going to take me. Maybe hell for all the naked strippers I lusted over and all the drinking I did.

Like most young men, college can be a defining point in life. I think I was lost. Now, I know I was lost. I met a girl and was dumb and stupid for involving her or me in a ridiculous relationship. I knew it as soon as I got in it but had a real problem exiting the relationship because I did not want to scar her life. I think the relationship only existed because of my loneliness, isolation, and lack of direction.

I met her in church camp. I was always involved in a church, even in El Paso, but I just could not get this reality of this Jesus guy in me like others seemed to accomplish. In looking at her life, it had never started, and it was not reasonable to continue a relationship of any kind. It started as fast as it ended. I have never seen her or talked to her until the afternoon that I departed El Paso, Texas. I have never heard of her since. I think I was lonely and saw no way to get into a decent relationship. I was working at a local hospital, and I soon learned that everyone was having sex with everyone else. It was a rough place to meet someone you could talk to and maybe open the door of emotions just a bit. It was usual for me to get an invitation to all the parties, but sex was rampant. It seemed all the old ugly horny divorced women from the business office were trying to get lucky with some of the young guys in the hospital. I just kept envisioning my mom. Crap!

Chapter 9
A Lucky Break or God?

Days have passed, and Kim was looking at going back to work after the holidays.

We went from having a few vacation days from our holiday to feeling glad it was over. I told Kim I needed to see my brothers, and I might try to see them. The off part of this was remembering traveling from El Paso, Texas, seeing my older brother, Ron, one Christmas while he was in Amarillo in pastoral training. I met a hospital director who was a friend he worked with at the hospital.

That man was the President of the National Association of Respiratory Therapy. He was like the King in the profession. I didn't think much about the meeting or anything else and went back to El Paso, Texas, after a short visit. A day later, the Director of Respiratory Therapy located me in the hospital, and she offered me a job. What! The President of the Respiratory Therapy Association called her and told her to hire me. I started the next day on the night shift and quickly worked alone, covering a hospital of sick kids and adults. Every part of me to the cells in my blood changed. I found my destiny in working with sick and fragile patients. I saw many patients ultimately die with an overwhelming impact on the deepest parts of my soul and heart. This job seemed to be my real ministry in life, not taking a bus full of Christian kids on a ski trip.

I will never forget a small Mexican boy in an oxygen croup tent. The tent was like being in a clear plastic tent with cool oxygen pumping into it because of his swollen windpipe. We had difficulty with the mom understanding that the TV remote could not be in the tent with her son because it had mechanical metal parts to operate the TV. If it had metal friction, it could blow up the tent and kill the kid. I checked on him regularly, and sort of fell in love with his mom and her child because she was poor but so loving and gentle. She would sleep in the croup tent to comfort her son. Can you sense what was going to happen next? The TV remote went click-click-click, and the tent blew up. Every alarm went off in the hospital, and I remember running into the room, and the tent and bed were nothing but fire. I did everything I could to get the oxygen gauge turned off to stop feeding the fire with oxygen. The fire engulfed the room because oxygen was flowing freely from the oxygen gauge. I finally turned off a zone valve in the hallway stopping the feed of oxygen to the open air in the room. Both mom and son died of massive burns.

I remember being in counseling a few years ago. I told my counselor after I had slowed down in my career that I was having a lot of toxic dreams. The dreams were as real as me breathing today, and I was in the middle of them. They were like re-winds of my life. I realized all the trauma and helicopter life flights made a significant impact on me. We never went through any sort of work debriefing in those days. We just dove into the burns, brains, guts, and blood and went on down the road and sucked it up. I remember telling my counseling therapist that I can remember five people I know I failed in their illness or injury. In those days, a Respirator or Ventilator looked like something from outer space than the old Iron Lungs that set the standard of care for years. Nonetheless of why - they all died with me at the bedside. I knew they had hopes I had the trick.

It was late at night, and I was in my office, unable to sleep.

To my counselor:

I found another one I had tucked away for over 50 years. You guessed it, the little boy and mom in the oxygen tent. He had brown eyes, brown hair and must have weighed 55 lbs., and his mom must have been in her late twenties. I brought him a truck at Walgreens Drug Store on my way to work for him to play within the crib because he had no toys. She couldn't speak any English words and was from Juarez, Mexico. I remember her smiles, warmth but behind her brown eyes was fear. She was poor with black hair, and she wore the same dress and moccasin shoes as she stayed by his side, never leaving him.

Obviously, over fifty years later, I remember both very clearly as though the accident happened today. To everyone else, it was just a Mexican woman across the border and her child with no husband. I didn't feel at blame, but I had never seen two people burn to death so engulfed in a fire there was no screaming. I can see other images of several of those that died as I type these very words over 50 years ago. I know I had something unique to offer because when I would work the night shift with those we knew were probably going to die, they seemed to light up when I came on my shift. What they didn't realize was that I was lonely, lacked purpose, and they seemed to fill a big void in my life. They all ended up dying on my work shift. I think we seemed to wait for each other.

I remember being off of work for a few days, and I went to work at midnight. I went up to the Intensive Care Unit. I had been taking care of a lady who had a degenerative muscle disease and was dying. The only thing keeping her alive was the ventilator. As I walked by the nursing unit, a favorite nurse of mine peered over her glasses and said, "She has been waiting for you to die." I remember glancing back at her, saying, "You're full of BS." She smiled back at me and said, "No, she won't die without you."

Before I could again tell her, she was full of it - I was at her bedside. She couldn't talk but used her lips real well to try and communicate. I remarkably could get most of what she said. I walked up and looked at her. She looked down at her hand because she couldn't move any part of her body. I knew she wanted me to hold her hand, and I grabbed it. I held it and said that I had missed her, and she smiled gently and tenderly at me. She said she wanted to say Goodbye to me. Before I cracked off with something corny, I looked at her eyes and knew she was going to quit. And she died holding my hand. I didn't realize my favorite nurse was standing close to me, watching, and walked over to me and hugged me. I just cried. I will never forget what she said. "Dave, you have a real gift and never get in a hurry at the bedside because you don't realize your effect on dying people who need your peace and joy." It still causes me to cry, thinking of the times I forgot her words.

In looking back, I know they felt safe with me to let go. All I remember is that it crushed me because each one dying was a loss for me. Work became my life. Years later, as my dad lay dying with hours to live, the family had gathered around my dad. It was late, and I told my brothers Kim and I would stay in the late part of the night. We would call them if anything happened. A little past 2:00 am, I was doing the care for my dad's mouth and lips and talking to him. I turned away and looked back from the side of my eyes and saw and heard him take his last breath. In afterthought, I knew he felt safe with me in going on to the Father. It was a good moment. My dad and I had talked about that moment in dying many times. The conversation always seemed to focus on what might be happening in the spiritual realm of the world. I knew when it was going to happen that it would be with me. Concerning all the brothers, I spent most of the time with dad as a son, an employee, and later living in the same town till his death.

Since I was the only therapist at night in El Paso, I was popular. The night supervisor liked me, and I liked her. She had worked nights for years. She sort of seemed like a mom but someone with whom I could eat breakfast and enjoy a cup of coffee. I remember right before I left El Paso that the black orderly was a prankster. A patient had died, and he asked me to help him take the body to the morgue. We decided that I should call the supervisor, and he should hide the corpse in another vault. I would open the door to the storage vault and pull out the stretcher, and he would rise and scream, "Booga Booga!" Well, we did that. She screamed bloody murder and hit the floor. She passed out with major stitches from a gash in the head.

It went from hilarious to "oh, hell!" The next day, he lost his job, and I got put on disciplinary probation. Mildly said, I was never going to have coffee with her nor ever tell her goodbye. That was a hard lesson for me to lose a warm friendship over a prank with someone I would ever have a relationship with or see again. I was the loser with a hard lesson in honoring and respecting friend relationships.

Months later, my boss got a call from the same man in Amarillo, Texas, the President of the National Respiratory Therapy Association. She told me they were starting a brand-new Respiratory Therapy School in Texas. It was in Amarillo, and the school was only taking five select individuals. By the way, tell Dave that he is accepted, and I have a job for him. Can he come tomorrow? Before I could think about it, my director told me to pack up my car and leave with her blessings. And I did. This move was God-ordained. I can't say I realized it was the hand of God until much later in life. Funny, I can't remember praying for my rescue or maybe even crying out during this entire disastrous time in El Paso. A Christian response had left me and took some years to regain. It was later I realized the time at El Paso was adding to a bag full of hurts. In hindsight, God was working in and around me despite my lack of relationship.

It was a classic example of a Christian bible story about Christ's disciples walking to a town called Emmaus after his crucifixion and Christ revealed himself. The disciples soon realized that Christ was with them all along in their journey, and they were unaware it was Him. Like them, I was clueless about the ever-presence of Him in my life. But wow! I was in the car driving to Amarillo!

Chapter 10
It Seemed Like God

In this part of my life, El Paso seemed like a blur and never existed even though I was in my senior year of college. In anticipating a career and being a youth pastor still seemed OK. Brite Divinity School had accepted me into seminary in Fort Worth, Texas. I could make that happen only to miss the whole point of being "called by God into ministry." I had this idea I could be a youth director. While in high school, I was a high school youth leader for a large section of Texas and preached in rural communities to help develop guys like me to be in ministry. What it probably did in retrospect was give me some self-esteem and be able to talk to any kind of people from the city to a rural community. It was exactly where I continue to live. My career has always emphasized a rural community.

I left El Paso, Texas, as though I was never there. The relationships with people were few as I was a wandering soul who simply vanished one day. I said goodbye to less than a handful of people and never looked back. There was regret in the decision to go the "opposite way" of my big brother. It was like I needed just to be me and not have much hanging over me. I knew going down the highway to El Paso, Texas, a place I never belonged. I had no support system, one friend, and no established networking with people. I knew I made a wrong decision, but by golly, I stuck with it. My dad always taught me to make a decision and stick with it. And I did.

I could not put my feelings into words as I didn't know how to sit and ask my dad what to do. Somewhere a voice went off in my head that I didn't have the freedom to do that. I never remember having family conversations and discussions about our family and goals. We did everything Dad told us to and never questioned him, and that was the sixties culture. I don't remember remorse, sadness, or joy driving off that day to college. I don't remember my dad being at home when I left for college. There was certainly no spam or tuna fish sandwiches with cookies.

It had been a ten-hour night-long road trip from El Paso, Texas, to my new home in Amarillo. I remember sitting blurry-eyed at the red light gazing out over this massive Baptist Hospital. I had no clue the impact this hospital would ultimately have on my life.

Years later, I am sitting at the same traffic light after getting gas on Christmas taking the administrative call for that same hospital. I am looking at this hospital with a torn-up family, and I am suddenly there again. My god, what was this all about?

We had a court date set for Brady, and things were suddenly getting real with Brady, Kim, and me. We discussed Brady was reaping the consequences of his action, and we decided not to hire an attorney for him. We knew this action could have ugly consequences. The court would appoint him an attorney. These attorneys were typically brand new attorneys with no real experience or old drunks who couldn't maintain a law practice. His attorney was a young guy starting his law practice trying to pick up some clients from the court system. I remember going to see him about the case. He reminded me quickly that Brady was eighteen years old, and the law considered him an adult.

I had no rights or much to say. Well, that is all I needed to hear that I, as the father had nothing to say. I think I said, or maybe I imagined saying, "I am fixing to come across the desk and knock you out – you young, smart-ass attorney!" He would be the second person that I was going to come across the desk and knock out – a preacher and a lawyer. What better two to knock out! But this young and new attorney got it in both barrels of how Brady was a good kid and did not need to go to the state prison. His life would be over. He was a friendly kid, but he heard what I had to say. I must admit that the conversation came from deep fear I would lose my kid to the Texas Prison System. I knew his life would be over. Brady had told me he would never make it to the prison. And what about me and my career. I had something to lose in this deal. Brady had screwed a lot of things up. Sure. It seemed it was all Brady's fault.

I got a job working as an evening EKG technician at that Baptist Hospital. I was grateful for the job and later went to the night shift as a Respiratory Therapist and quickly worked alone, responsible for the entire hospital. At this point in life, I had five years of college with only an associate degree. Here I was investing two more years in another associate college degree. The difference was I found my calling. I knew my calling was saving lives and comforting death more times than I could ever count. I was truly in my place. Soon, I found the same church denomination I grew up in and quickly started teaching junior high school Sunday school.

I remember one thing about those days – I lived in an icebox called an apartment. In those days, Amarillo, Texas, had blizzards and icy, frigid weather. I had no idea what I had left from hot and sandy West Texas. Suddenly I was in the Texas Panhandle, where it was hot in the morning, and there could be snow at night. I found school very easy and natural because everyone who was a student was working at the same hospital. All "five" of us had worked in hospitals across the southwest. We were a great group. We were probably the model bunch of misfits. We certainly were favorites in the hospital with nurses and doctors. We had no idea we were "trailblazing" a new era into medicine in Amarillo and the Texas Panhandle. There was only this school and one more, and we were it.

In those days, iron lungs were considered the standard of giving breath to someone. The "other" hospital in town did not have a department, and they used iron lungs, and whatever would pump air into someone. We never went to that hospital for clinical experience. It was old, awful, and backward. Our hospital had the beginning technology of modern ventilators with the only board-certified pulmonary doctor. He loved us, and we loved him, and we were just a great team. I can remember almost everything to this day and some of the patients I treated. It was a confirmation that I found not only my profession but my calling in ministry. I was beginning to understand that "saving lives" in the Intensive Care Unit, in the skies, or Emergency Room was as good as it got. I was beginning to have a "story" and could share who I was with patients and nurses late at night. I realized I might have a more significant impact on my job than a youth director or preacher. My self-image was growing, and my size and lack of money did not affect me. I was in a brand new and upcoming field in medicine. I primed at what seemed the best time of my life. In those days, it seemed natural to be married and have a kid before you turned twenty. For me, at twenty, I jumped around in school and was clueless as to my real passion.

On the night shift or other shifts on the weekend, I had the advantage of being all over the hospital in different departments and nursing units. I figured out which nurse I might have the best chance of getting a date. I didn't have a lot of money, and I really didn't dance or drink anymore. I mean, a walk in the park isn't someone's best idea of a date. I had a few dates with a few beautiful nurses. I began to understand that I had value, and I was not the "service station guy" anymore. I also realized that hospitals could be very rough, with flirty nurses and folks messing around. Our five respiratory students had many lonely older nurses think we were a pretty hot catch for a short one-night stand. For the life of me, I couldn't quite get my head wrapped around going to bed with someone my mom's age. I also found out that hospital night shifts were a whole new world with people and late-night activities. I think there were more sexually aroused older nurses than younger ones. Maybe that was because older and divorced, or widow ladies worked the night shift. I got more "touches" in a room by nurses trying to "get something for the patient" than I could imagine. I must tell you that it became a fantasy for me to think about at night when I slept alone in my apartment.

I know I had those fantasies come from my first brushes with pornography. When we were kids and had to wash clothes and put them away, I remember opening my dad's sock and underwear drawer and found some naked girl magazines. By today's standards, I might have been looking in the bra section of the Victoria Secret catalog – which I did. In looking back, the seed of pornography got me. My dad was looking at naked women's pictures. I don't remember judging him or thinking ill of him because he opened a whole new door for me. Oddly, in junior high school, I had stacks of magazines in my closet, and I found myself stealing Playboy magazines at the corner grocery store.

I remember my mom was vacuuming the closet one Saturday morning. I thought I had the magazines well hid in a zip-up clothes bag. She told me when she bumped into the bag with the vacuum machine, she heard a thud and looked inside. There must have been 40 Playboy magazines. I came home that day, and they were all on the bed. My mom never said a word to me. Crap! I got caught! I threw them away and stayed embarrassed until I stole my next magazine at the corner grocery. It seemed like a badge of courage with the guys looking at naked women at overnight sleep-ins. In those days, all you saw was thinly clothed models, but it allowed your imagination to go toxic. I think there was a deeper issue.

Growing up, I had no idea my male hormone was a problem until later diagnosed with medical tests. I had a low male image of myself because of my size and lack of penis size or body hair. My mom would always say that I was slick because of my Indian heritage from my dad. That was a good reason I could hold onto in my mind. I knew some things weren't right because in sports when everyone was getting dressed, I knew I didn't stack up. It was a huge issue because when friends talked about masturbating or walking around with their penis bulging, I couldn't find mine. That was a problem for me with girls and a male self-image. So, I had my world with naked girl's magazines. It also probably kept me a virgin because I feared being with a girl and wanting to "go all the way." I knew I probably didn't have what it took. What a dilemma! It seemed my self-image got better when I moved to Amarillo to school.

There is no question, "the five" flirted for food from the nurses on a nursing unit. The cafeteria was closed on the night shift, and if you didn't bring food, you didn't eat. There was no way any of "the five" would cook. We found certain nurses with reputations for getting flirty. When we were treating a patient, we had to coordinate our care with the patient's nurse. It was always a plan to be in the patient room at the same time if she was a prized nurse. I think I rehearsed my opening comment or checked my hair before going into the room more than I would like to think. It was a perfect setup with a flirty nurse, later known as horny, and a bunch of flirty guys, later known as horny. I think two of them had some wild encounters after work with the "older nurses." I liked the idea of it from the porno magazine articles. Still, I knew I probably sexually could not match up. It stayed a mental picture and not an action. However, I never saw how the early seed of pornography was real to me. Of course, I would justify that I was single, free, and had few responsibilities. The nagging voice in the back of my head, even in the days of Juarez, Mexico, was my dad telling me never to have sex with a girl and hold yourself for that special girl you would marry. The problem with that was you couldn't say to a bunch of guys because of being viewed as queer or some Jesus freak. What they didn't know was it was a combination of sexual performance and values. I knew from the many stories that I was the only one brought up in a church.

Chapter 11
I Finally Got a Rhythm

My experience grew and matured in the field of Respiratory Therapy. I soon found myself very good at patient care. I understood the therapy goal for every patient. It was like I could visualize the diseases within the body and the tools to care for the disease remarkably well. I never let myself admit how good I was, but I knew I was very gifted.

I found myself winning much favor with the department director, where he offered me a management job to stay after graduation. I hit the jackpot of all jobs. During that time, I got involved with my church. I was the eighth-grade Sunday school teacher, and we had a great classroom with no chairs, carpet, and bean bags on the floor. I had a reputation for being a cool teacher. The church choir director requested me to go with the youth choir to a major world convention in Mexico City as a youth sponsor. I was thrilled. I remember getting my director to approve the trip and somehow got all the money lined up. I would remind him of the days I needed to be absent closer it came to the departure.

On my last time reminding him two weeks before the trip, he looked right at me and said I couldn't go. He gave me no reason. He tried to just walk off from our conversation, but I reminded him of our discussions and commitments. He just looked at me and said he was sorry he had committed to me. I saw myself go "out of body" with my response to him. It was not pretty. I knew from my past working for my dad how to respond appropriately. I knew I was lied to and deceived. Well, my days of being the Number Two guy got numbered fast. I suddenly found myself in a bad spot. The other hospital was an absolute disaster and had the worst medical staff and facility in America. They didn't even have oxygen and suction in the patient rooms, and this was the place that used Iron Lungs and did not have a department. I knew what injustice was working with the porters in the service stations. I had learned to do the right things in life, but this hit me in the face of that word injustice. Suddenly, I was faced with nowhere to work because I couldn't stay there with what happened to me.

To my surprise, the old hospital hired a well-trained respiratory therapist. The hospital decided to establish a department. I got a call to talk to the new director. He got my name from the school because my class rating was the top student with previous job experience. Even more, I worked at the Baptist hospital, and that was a plus. He hired me on the spot. I was beyond excited. I had no clue what the future would hold for me at that hospital. A potentially terrible problem suddenly got better.

It was at this phase of my life and career that life was never the same. I had graduated; I was good, single, and was an Assistant Director of a large city hospital. I had met a girl whose folks were also Sunday school teachers for the high school students. She was a petite blonde and quite shy. I later learned she knew more about me because I had treated her mother at the Baptist Hospital. She would later tell me she would rush to get to the hospital with a chance of seeing me when I treated her mom while hospitalized with a broken hip. She had long blonde hair down to her butt, and I never paid much attention to her. However, one day she cut her hair to what they called a short wedge. I asked her out for a date that day I saw her with a new haircut. It was hard to think it was the same girl.

Even though I was at the "worst hospital, maybe on the planet," I saw it as an excellent opportunity to build something from scratch. Because of my inner hurts and injustice at the Baptist Hospital, I vowed to beat them in everything. We would have the premier respiratory therapy department even amid an old antiquated hospital. I didn't give it much thought, but I was in a sense back in West Texas at the service station letting the rich beat me or have more than me – which was the Baptist Hospital. I know it was the energy of winning or being better. I rarely spoke it out loud, but it was the fuel in the engine.

The great thing about being at this hospital was my brother had finished his hospital chaplaincy certification. He was starting a new chaplain department. We were at the same place working. What I soon realized was this hospital had a vision to "get into the future." Their vision included a new hospital next to the Baptist Hospital in a newly developed medical center. That didn't occupy my thinking because I was in a hell hole with no technology, awful and backward doctors, and no one understood what we did as a profession. For all, they knew we just hauled around giant oxygen bottles and were oxygen technicians. Many times, I felt I was in a bad dream.

My director was probably the nicest guy in the world. It was probably good timing because I was younger and had worked in nice and modern hospitals. I could come out of the gate at a second's notice. We were a good pair because he was more politically correct, and I had no idea what that meant. I just knew I seemed to compliment him. I learned a lot about patience and communication. He was friendly, complimentary, and was gently establishing a department. I was sort of the young kid he needed to get it done at the bedside. We made a good team, and we started with an incredible task. I was up for the job, as was he. I knew he was a Christian as he went to the Baptist church, and he knew my church background of teaching Sunday school. I guess that was my definition of a Christian.

I found out he was a reserve in the Army, and he had to go to Oklahoma for Army reserve training each summer. I felt prepared to take over the department while he was gone. We were beginning to "weed out" some of the old employees that simply hauled oxygen bottles from room to room. They were good guys but had no clue where we were going, and being certified in the field was a mandate. So, we created jobs just for them, and they seemed happy. To them, work was a check and a six-pack of beer after work.

I will not forget a call I got from the Assistant Administrator over my department. He was as crazy as hell. He had been a nurse, and he climbed to the top, breaking every rule that existed, and it seemed to fit him well. He was ahead of his time because he thought and worked as a twenty-first-century hospital executive. He smoked cigarettes like a freight train. I never heard him not curse. He also had uncontrolled diabetes because he couldn't stay married and eat correctly and could not keep his sugar levels stable. He would stand his ground against anything. I liked him a lot because I could identify with a similar rebellious spirit. The call to me was that my Director was involved in a major wreck on the Army base and left him in a vegetative state. I remember him not missing a heartbeat and said, "Clark, make it happen." I had a moment to be sad, and then every engine turned on. The Director ended up living for many years but never was physically or mentally the same again. Amid his tragedy, he checked on me frequently. I attended his funeral several years ago. My dad would say that God ordained every action for a perfect purpose, and I began to see that.

OK, wow! Dave is in charge. I am the Director. I have hit my goal. I had arrived. Wow, this is great. Hell, I have never done this! The same respiratory school I had attended was putting out many graduates. It took about two years, and the Baptist Hospital could no longer hire all the top graduates. The timing seemed perfect because we were beginning to overcome a past reputation. We had the Baptist Hospital in our sights. So, I suddenly had a pool of therapists, and I was hiring them like crazy. I put all my past experiences in gear and started throwing out Iron Lungs and all these antiques and giving them to museums. I fought with some of the meanest, dumbest and hateful doctors on the planet. I came from a hospital with an esteemed pulmonary doctor. I was in a place with a bunch of what I just have to call idiot doctors whom I knew were prematurely sending folks to their graves with their ignorance. I saw more patients removed from life support and just laid there suffocating because the doctor had decided it was over. It devastated me. I was watching a handful of doctors not give a damn and just walk by and turn off a ventilator and go to lunch. Everyone was too intimidated and scared to confront them, but I did. My boss and I stood our ground, and we started changing things from the nursery to the emergency room. A funeral home operated the local ambulance service. It sort of made sense, and it was symbolic because patients died in the ambulance before getting to the hospital.

The most significant gift my boss ever did for me was life and career-changing – he trusted me, saw my heart, and sent me out with bullets in a gun. We made major changes in an old beat-up Emergency Room to what became a major trauma center. I found myself figuring out how to coordinate the communication of a 26 county Emergency System. This system became the first mark of my career. It was natural for me to start thinking about systems management. Soon, we had a coordinated ambulance and helicopter system and communication system plus a paramedic school I co-taught. We went from nothing to something fast. I worked with an aggressive and equally crazy Emergency Department Director, Virginia Scott, and an EMS Executive Director, Betty O'Rourke. We became a fantastic team changing the culture and landscape of medicine in an entire region bigger than most states in our country. Moreover, we had a neurosurgeon who served as our medical advisor who got the whole picture, Dr. Louis Finney, who was aggressive and maybe a bit warped and crazy. I later gave his eulogy at this funeral. We recruited a recognized ambulance service, and we did aggressive pre-hospital care. I suddenly was evolving more than a Respiratory Therapy Director. We soon hired a shock trauma physician team, which radicalized the Intensive Care Unit and Surgical Services. Ha! We ran off the bad doctors and brought in the lifesavers, and suddenly we were crazy good.

Yes, there were screaming and hollering threats with near fists in the hallways, and it seemed my life got threatened more than I knew. No one could hurt me. Remember, I had the Head of the God Squad on my side - my brother and his chaplains. We suddenly became better than the Baptist Hospital. Therapists were clamoring to get into our department because we had a helicopter service, an active emergency room, and many critical patients. I had my bunch in the very middle of it. Just occasionally, I would smile going down the hallway, knowing I had kicked the Baptist pretty hard. Their reputation was considered the Country Club, and we were the Knife and Gun Club. Everybody gowned up as blood and guts would fly, and we were at our best. But some things began to happen at home.

I married that short-haired blonde, Kim. I remember taking her up to the Newborn Nursery and walked her through the hospital like a proclaiming warrior, saying, this is what I do. In other words, this had my heart—a big problem.

Chapter 12
Maybe Foreshadowing, But Maybe God After All

While all the adult care was growing crazy, I remembered that on the third floor of the hospital was a nursery with premature babies. They were placed in a warm incubator hoping for the best. Most all the small or premature babies seemed to die. It devastated me. So, like adult care, we started hiring pediatricians from a university medical school in Kansas. We knew we needed a Neonatal ICU of some kind, and it seemed to fall back on me. I had started advocating the use of infant ventilators. To my surprise, one of the very attempts to use it came with my premature niece.

Kim Merriman was a young girl who was a senior in high school. She was cute, shy, a great singer, and somebody that caught my attention. I just had not been attracted to a girl with long hair, split down the middle, and that was it. Her parents were the Sunday school teachers at the church I attended when moving from El Paso, Texas. The crazy thing is the Youth Director in El Paso moved to Amarillo as an Associate Pastor. That made things a bit better, even though we didn't have much of a relationship outside the church. Kim's parents had a very successful local family grocery store. The store had been in the family for many years with an incredible reputation for quality beef and specialty products. It had the old-style market while you watched your beef get cut right in front of you. It was the store you could call in your order, have it delivered to your house, and charge it to your family account. It was "the" store you shopped in Amarillo. They had the market on the more affluent in town. Funny, that was the same as our family business, but we sold gas and tires. Her parents were warm and friendly and something very different about them. I didn't date Kim until she graduated from high school, but I didn't wait too long. I knew I was older, but that did not bother me. When the Brady fire hit, and we were in opposite camps on handling the situation, she would often ask me why I married her. I did not doubt my love, and she loved me. Kim was probably my first love. She was a petite, blonde, great family, a Christian, and had a great smile and a great body. She seemed to accept me for who I was and how I was. We spent a lot of time not doing anything fancy or cost-prohibitive because I didn't have it, and it didn't seem to matter. In retrospect, I didn't have a great impression of myself. It was later that a simple lab test would have made an enormous difference in my life as a boy, teen, and young man. That was the whole pituitary issue. Kim suffered from a poor self-image, and neither of us had a grip about any of that. Later in life, with Brady's problems, did I realize our marriage had to be ordained because both of us did everything to destroy our marriage.

Looking back over my marriage's early years, I think I acted like many men, with things gradually changing in the marriage. Some things were often not discussed, but it seemed like foreshadowing when I took Kim to the hospital with me when we were dating. I would often get paged out to the nursery for a sick baby. I reminded her, "this is my life." I remember one night on call; she came with me to the nursery. As we walked up to the nursery, it seemed every baby was on a ventilator and in critical condition. Suddenly, the nursery seemed like a significant neonatal ICU. It would prove a downfall in my personal life. We seemed to get out less on "dates," and being on call with a hospital pager for anything critical was common. The one problem in setting up a new department and trying to establish its identity and consistency meant being there when anything out of the ordinary occurred. At first, wearing a "pocket pager" seemed to be a "badge of honor" for key staff and doctors. It was rare to see folks in the community with a pager. You would automatically know it had to be a critical person at a hospital.

I must admit that I wore it with pride even though every night and weekend, it was going off, requiring me to get to the hospital. The last thing I wanted to do is make everyone dependent on "hero Dave" galloping into the hospital to save the day. Yeah, that felt good for a while until the gallop began to wear out. In a quick time, it was about getting to the hospital to teach and mentor staff more than anything else. I appointed some shift supervisors who were very talented and smart. I must admit we were excellent and committed. In time, they would carry the pager for the esteem of it because overtime pay was not even a known opportunity. Slowly, I began to build a team that was less dependent on me, and when they did call me, I knew all hell was happening.

I wish I could pinpoint when fear found its way into my life. After our marriage, I know I feared losing my job and not having money. There was absolutely no reason for that because I was the new young star at the hospital. Kim was working for her father as a bookkeeper. I knew she had to do something with school, but we wanted to make sure that when we had kids that she could be at home. Do you hear the flash drive kicking in with a message? No kids of mine were going to be raised by daycare and not have a mom at home.

On the other hand, the idea of no job terrified me that everything was on my shoulders as to work and money. I was making $6.33 an hour and felt like I was on top of the world. That is absolutely silly compared to the same job today.

It was only one night in a near helicopter crash that my fear was not being killed but crippled and unable to work. Then what would happen? Kim had to get into college.

When we got married, we rented my brother's house. They had moved to Dallas, Texas, for more education with his chaplaincy training. It was a great deal having a furnished home as it gave us time to find our house, save money, and get a start. It was a great gift that gave me tremendous relief that I could get a place to live.

Kim and I had grown up in the same church denomination, and it seemed Ok with me. There had been a program at the church called Lay Renewal Weekend. Kim will say that her dad got dramatically saved that weekend, and everything about his life changed. He would

Maybe Foreshadowing. But Maybe God After All

later become a pastor at what was one of the largest churches in the Texas Panhandle. Her folks were deeply spiritual. When I would evaluate a personal report card of me and my faith, it seemed I was missing something. We had decided we probably needed to find a church and start fresh after our marriage. I became very curious about what their folks had experienced. I knew me, or no one in our family had anything like that. They seem to have joy and happiness. They called it the Baptism of the Holy Spirit. Later I found out that this era in church history in the United States was called the Charismatic Movement. People would describe it as an outpouring of the Holy Spirit. I was clueless. Kim dragged me off to a bible study on the Holy Spirit at a local Catholic Church. I mean, here I am sitting in a catholic church. I knew not to say No this early in our marriage, and so I went.

My eyes got blasted open.

I must admit somewhere deep in me that I knew there had to be something more than my prior church experience. After sitting in a weekly night class for over six weeks, I got educated about this Holy Spirit deal. I was very resistant. All I knew about the Holy Ghost was in some liturgical phrase at the communion table. We said Father, Son, and Holy Ghost and drank some artificial grape juice and ate a cracker with something about this is the blood and body of Christ. Great. The short story of this was that we went to the Chapel one night after the class. Maybe I should say Kim stopped me from just going to the car. She could go and tell me about it. It was all about an opportunity to receive this Holy Spirit. I had to be the most skeptical and resistive human in the universe because it was so out of my church's traditional safe zone. Despite seeing and hearing my wife's parents and friends, I could not get my head wrapped around it. I mean, these were just ordinary people like me and not crazy, far-out Christians. How did I miss this in my entire church history? Short story, Kim and I both laid on the floor sort of dazed, speaking in some unknown language. Holy God. Well, that started a whole other chapter in our life.

Has this freaked you out yet? Well, it freaking did me.

Suddenly, the book has twisted into somewhat of a spiritual realm. If that is bothering you, I will say again, keep reading. I can hear you saying that you knew it. This guy was going to get God. And then the whole world flipped, and he was suddenly a great husband and father. Isn't that the way most good stories end? It may not turn out to be like you think with the sun rising, and the world is aglow with life and majesty and glory. Praise God, and I am out of here. Stay with me. If you look at the page number of this book, you have got to think there is something more or we are finished. The Clark family all got this Holy Spirit thing. Life is good. Nope. It didn't work that way. Keep reading.

Things in my family had begun to change with my mom and dad operating several nursing homes in West Texas. They decided to move to a small country town in Central Texas, where my dad moved to build and operate a new nursing home. My little brother was growing up with pimples, a scrawny physique, and virtually was a single child living with mom and dad. When they moved, it seemed right for him as he got out in the country and had a great opportunity to be a rural kid. I know he didn't like the elementary school he attended. It was the oldest elementary school in town, and it looked like a prison. It seemed all good for him. He was a great punter in football but got injured with a shoulder injury requiring major surgery. He played in the band, and when all that was not happening, he was raising hell in his own way. He had some great buddies that remain best friends today, with many experiencing their tragedies with a few divorces and deaths in between.

I know things didn't seem to change with my dad or Steve. After all, there didn't seem to be a need to do anything else. My dad would often call Ron and me because he wanted us to come home to "straighten him out." Guess what? The same hell with my big brother was going off with my little brother, Steve. Steve was just a small kid when Ron was at home due to the age differences. It wasn't like a video going off with Steve, but it was for my dad. There were rebellions and adversities everywhere. I knew Ron had it figured out. It might have been a lot of Steve, but it was my dad's anger. It was obvious dad never dealt with his issues with Ron and just kept piling on bad behavior. It seemed the Ron stuff just got carried over to Steve. I guess my one advantage is that "short guys" could fit in foxholes when bullets flew.

Maybe Foreshadowing. But Maybe God After All

Steve ran away from home at seventeen years old, writing mom and dad a goodbye letter marrying a sixteen-year-old high school girlfriend who was also running from family. They ended up running off to Mexico. There wasn't much time between marriage and finishing school with a new baby coming along. His wife came from a different culture from our family. It was apparent her mom would not be playing cards on Saturday night with my folks. Her mother later died from cancer. So, the Clarks go into the "save the day" drill again, trying to 'fix' this mess and somehow get Steve into school and college. We suddenly witnessed the same problem jump up in our home from an older brother. In Steve's case, his marriage seemed to wreck through seven years with a little boy and girl. The critical issue here is the repeating family history that is very important to note. Gosh, we had another "re-run" in the Clark family. It seemed generational behavior kept finding its way into all levels of our family. Dad never gave up on Steve or any of his sons despite a toxic circling effect on parenting.

My dad was a successful nursing home administrator and organizing an effort to close a failing doctor's clinic. He was an alcoholic with all the pitfalls of that disease. Dad formed an ambulance service and operated the county hospital district later to recruit and hire a doctor from Viet Nam. The doctor was quite good and thriving in a tiny rural Texas town. He later organized a county ambulance service to meet the needs of that rural county.

For all these things, dad was quite the guy. At this point, our home life did not have a good batting average. We all knew things weren't right, but we couldn't just say that our dad was violent, short-tempered and our mother was a manipulator, and "the Clark family" was all OK. It took my two brothers and me quite a while to work through life traumas that were coming down that railroad track, smoking and blasting out its horns. Of course, we didn't hear the horns and worked out of the behavior habits and mannerisms we saw and experienced at home. Who would know to do any different?

My marriage took off well with me, digging in the hospital and Kim working for her dad. We eventually rented a house from an older man who was friendly and accommodating. We started buying paint, and I think our kitchen went to a bright lime color, which seemed to be the trend. We purchased furniture from friends having garage sales or were just getting rid of furniture downsizing their homes. I remember buying our first living room tables from White's Auto Store in a small furniture section. I later found out it was fabricated wood with plastic doors, but they looked real enough for our house. We paid cash because we wanted no debt. The motivating drive was my fear of owing anyone money. I worried about losing my job and if I could pay my bills. My dad had taught us never to have debt. I was teaching at the local college where the extra money went to buying furniture, a lawnmower, and all those essentials of family and house.

I had a sporty yellow Volkswagen I had in college. It seemed to be a real icon with special tire hubs and a special exhaust system. It sounded like a hot rod. It was cool. It seemed to fit Kim and me really well with a sporty look. With ideas of a family, we sold it and upstaged to a four-door Lincoln vehicle. The paint later peeled off, but it had a beautiful cloth interior, electric windows, and new car luxuries. It was sort of that family car with a pricy look. Our yard was perfect because that was a standard in our childhood of pretty grass, flowerbeds, and everything trimmed. Our backyard was a monster. It had a funny-looking grass later described as a Bind Weed that grew clear to hell and spread like a virus.

I later found it was a common and terrible weed growing on the side of Texas highways. It would take the worst poison on the planet to kill. This weed was living in my backyard of all places. How could I look out the kitchen window and not see a perfect backyard? I had this vision; it would come from under the house into our house and strangle us in the middle of the night. I didn't know the more you mowed it, the more it grew. I eventually gave up, and we moved to our first home. It was the home of our first son, Brady, and he had a warm and cozy nursery. At this time of our marriage, we decided that Kim would be a stay-at-home mother to raise our kids as much as possible. I don't think I ever gauged the effect on me with only one check. What if I lost my job?

During that time, a phenomenon occurred with babies across the United States called SIDS or Sudden Infant Death Syndrome. It frequently happened even with healthy babies who would die in their sleep. The baby, for some reason, just quit breathing, and unnoticed in the night would result in death. Because I was really involved in the newborn nursery, I had to respond to the Emergency

Maybe Foreshadowing. But Maybe God After All

Room for any critical call. There I saw several of our full-term babies in the Emergency Room and, for some reason, just quit breathing. I had to resuscitate them, and most were dead before EMS arrived. It had a profound effect on me. That is when I started a SIDS Home Monitoring Program at the hospital where we tried to run "sleep studies" on what seemed to be high-risk kids. We would give them low doses of caffeine to stimulate breathing. It was like throwing a needle at a haystack. I became so paranoid that I would sleep on the floor below Brady's crib at night (hoping the weed wouldn't come through the floor and kill me).

What I didn't realize about fathering at this early stage of being a father was learning to be a Provider and Protector. It seemed easy for me because my dad did a good job demonstrating having a job to provide for your family and having a home for safety. I had my home, a rent house, my yard, a new car, a baby, and a pretty wife. Along with that was a deep fear of losing my job. It scared me to death. I knew my parents didn't have the kind of money to help if something happened. Wow, I was in the middle of this father, husband, provider, and protector deal.

Things seemed real normal with Brady growing, and suddenly yard work was more of a hobby. Then we grilled meat on Saturday evening with our first barbeque pit, which was nothing but a big 50-gallon drum with a hole cut in it with welded iron for legs. It was cool and worked well. Our barbeque pit growing up was a big steel pot with legs and a lid that Casey inherited. Nothing of any family value or memory was ever taken to the trash or given away. Casey inherited the pit his pampa used when I was a boy. It is still much of a tradition to have backyard cookouts with steaks, barbeque chicken, and cold beer – a Texas thing.

I had never been a husband and father, and all I knew to do was remember what I saw my dad do or watch my brother, who lived in the same town. Guys, this is how we learned to be dads. If I were brave, I would ask my dad certain things. But I had to make sure he knew I was OK and knew what I was doing. It seemed most of the time; it was how to fix something or to talk about work. I never had a conversation of "how is it going with you and Kim?" or "How are you doing with Brady being a Dad…. what can I do to help you miss some pitfalls?" It was almost like the book he gave me on sex, but this didn't come with a book. There were no times that he and I would sit on the porch and talk about being a dad. I guess the idea was I was supposed to know what to do. I learned how to run a service station at 16 years old but few tools to be a dad.

The figures on divorce today in America reveal a divorce rate of over 52%. If statistics were available, it would be higher in Africa and most likely lower in Pakistan due to strong Muslim standards. The prevalence of infidelity in marriages is off the chart. That is my generation of fathers. Those statistics did not miss our families on both sides of the aisle. It confirms that those pretty and nice church families are as much into infidelity as the non-church families. Our families and marriages were not an exception. See what I meant earlier when I said, "life is a wonderful glow after a spiritual conversion?" My advice is to come back and talk to me after your moment of glow after a few months to see how it is going. In no way am I trying to throw water on your fire. Generally, we do a poor job of instructing people because it takes a lot of wood and people to help keep that fire glowing. I guess I missed that one.

Work was about getting better, and I got stronger in confidence and skills. Whenever a new hospital project at the hospital came up, my boss gave it to me. We were modernizing the department. We soon became a Beta site or test site for new ventilators on the market because of our diversity of patients we received with trauma, premature babies, and sick kids. It seemed like a MASH unit. We were the central hospital in 26 counties for all emergency care. To reference the area's size, it was bigger than many states in America and other countries in Africa, Europe, or the Middle East.

During that time, I noted the Ambulance Service was a "grab and run" service with minimal care. You got the patient in the back of an ambulance and ran to the hospital, giving little or no care. It made me nuts that patients could have lived if better training and resources were made available. I found myself on a committee to determine how to obtain a professional paramedic service for our city. In time, we hired a service, and things dramatically changed with excellent care in our cities' streets. Our Emergency Room hired some nationally known Shock Trauma Specialists. We formed a system of ambulances, hospitals, and communications all networked into our hospital. It later gained national prominence in an organized

Emergency Medical System. Wow, we had one heck of a paramedic program that won several state awards. I was right in the middle of all its teaching, training, and sitting on boards. Suddenly, I was speaking at national meetings as an expert. Good, God! And we were damn good. We were like a "Special Forces" team coming at you. We had a life-changing group of young men women in the middle of highways and homes, saving lives, talking to doctors from the scene of an accident, and sending heart scans through the airways. We were ahead of our time with extraordinary young men and women. They were champions of emergency care. Many left to lead major roles in off-shore drilling care, life-flight services, doctors, nurses, and nurse practitioners. Amazing. However, it sucked the life from me.

What this meant on the home front was even more time away from home. My weekends were full of training rural ranchers, business owners, and firefighters to save lives as EMS volunteers in a rural region bigger than most countries. We lacked one thing – a helicopter. Crap! Who was going to do that, and how and who? Me.

Developing one of the first helicopter programs in Texas was a life-changing and career-changing project. Suddenly we are flying the Texas skies in a used Viet Nam medivac helicopter used by the local sheriff department. We had a program, and history began. Suddenly this kid was in a helicopter with no training or clue how to resuscitate in a loud, vibrating helicopter. We flew night and day. It was a defining time in my life and career. And more time away from home. You see, in my mind, without thinking of it in these terms, I was building an incredible resume of job stability and assurance. They would never fire me, and they didn't. I had the reputation that if you needed something, even maybe a little crazy, call Clark.

Soon the court set a date for Brady's hearing. The reality of Brady going to the State Prison was very real. I remember investigating every possible program for Brady to be sentenced to, including a ship off the Texas coast. They took kids repeatedly in trouble with the law and taught them to work and complete their high school education. However, a local program designed after a national Christian program for troubled teens was in Amarillo and free. We began to see many resources going toward Brady to get him well would put a complete financial strain on the family.

I remember the sentence of seven years of probation, and Brady entered the Life Challenge Rehab Program. It was voluntary even though we asked the judge to make it mandatory. We knew if Brady had his choice, he would leave at the first opportunity. Brady's attitude in the courtroom was what I might describe as afraid but cocky. It seemed he couldn't quite interpret how serious this was and the work behind the scenes to help him. Even after the judge sentenced him, he reversed his mandatory rehab sentence to voluntary. He instructed Brady that any "falling off the mark" would result in going to the state prison. In looking back, I knew it was more of a scare tactic than anything else, but Brady went to the program for eighteen months. I asked the judge and program director if we could take Brady home from the court that day as we had never had Christmas with him. We had a dead Christmas tree and his presents still under the tree. From our living room in our house, we took him straight to the rehab. It was more than an afternoon of mixed feelings. When we left him there, they said we could not see him for a minimum of three months. I think we finally were oddly relieved that he was at least safe, and it was a chance for something.

Chapter 13
When Does This Ever Get Better?

It was a long season of time. Brady and I learned it was a healing time for him and me. We both journeyed to "places" spiritually that otherwise, we would not have typically experienced. We both knew we had to make radical changes. And we did. I was unaware that Kim was falling into further despair.

During this time, I attended a men's bible or fellowship group with some guys who convinced me to get up once a week at 6:00 am and talk religious stuff. Good Grief! But I did because I found a group of similar misfits that seem to be honest about their families and kids. We remained together well over five years through personal tragedies, divorces, and marital affairs. We could probably label ourselves as "up-standing, aloof, not so poor, Christian, good looking, successful but walking disasters." At that time, the guys asked me to attend a "Walk to Emmaus," a non-denominational gathering at a retreat center for three days. It was sort of but not like a church men's retreat. The central theme of The Walk to Emmaus® is a spiritual renewal program intended to strengthen the local church by developing Christian disciples and church leaders. I would encourage you to go onto the web: emmaus.upperroom.org and investigate this as it became the transforming catalyst that changed my life – as it has for millions of men and women worldwide. It was the most profound life-changing experience I ever expected. I refused to go on two other occasions, and I think the third time, they gagged me and threw me in the trunk of the car to get me there. I could hear them say, "Good luck with this guy. You will need it with him."

Ok, guys, this is where this story takes a different direction. I am beginning to see or add up my life like sitting in a widescreen theater with a Dolby sound system. I had to start to admit, as painful as it would prove to be for me, that I had to get past some of my stuff that was toxic to my thinking and wrong thinking. This stuff was hurting me. As you will see, I still held at bay the spiritual component. The guy growing up in the church was having issues. As I travel and talk to all walks of men, I have begun to think that guys without any spiritual background or bad baggage get through this time better. It seems you have to re-program guys like me with a new hard drive to get past all the suitcases of baggage you grew up with, and they didn't either seem to fit or work for any good reasons. I had to begin to soften myself, and you know something? What did I have to lose? Take a risk on changing or stay in the place of misery I have been sitting for years with fear, anger, and disappointment. My report card wasn't so hot. So, I finally said, "What the hell."

It was the most incredible experience for me to see the Body of Christ so profoundly. I had never seen anything like a church service or religious event like these three days. I guess you might say I finally found Christ. It happened in a way I could accept and internalize from the day of being that fourth-grader on Easter Sunday, accepting Christ. I found myself turned inside and out. I could dedicate a book to that weekend and the dozens of weekends that I volunteered, directed, and subsequently trained Emmaus teams for other walks. That experience was in 1996, and I still refer to it twenty-five years later. It continues influencing the life changes in my behavior patterns. I found similar men who had similar life issues. They were willing to help navigate me and help me to trust in releasing my hurt, pain, and anger to the fullness of the Holy Spirit. I am not trying to scare you into thinking I am some religious zealot. Far from it. I understood the term "being delivered, and in the depth of my soul, I experienced something different with the Holy Spirit. Let me take you inside that event for a few days. Remember, it is not the event but my attitude we are talking about right now.

Ok, I will sit at a table with a bunch of other guys for three days sharing parts of our life, and go home on the third day – done. Are you guys happy with that? I will admit I hated it until the last hours of the second day. I realized those who asked me to go and those men I sat with for those three days were exactly like me. They had been hurt, messed up, divorced, kids in prison, and the list nearly made me throw up in the trash can next to the table I sat. I remember saying, "these guys are really messed up – funny." Always projecting outward. There was absolutely nothing all that special. I just got to sit with a few guys for a few days and learn that I was not alone, and I should consider saying Yes as they did, and I did.

Well, my anger showed through vividly. I couldn't deny I was mad at Kim, Brady, job, life, parents, relatives, church, and I was just an unhappy guy. But I was the happy, charismatic community and hospital leader to everyone who said hello to me. Dave was hurt, crushed, disappointed, angry, alone, and even my simple Sunday School teachings as a child about God is love and forgiveness failed me. I quickly moved all of this to the side. I needed to be loved and forgiven. Yes, that weekend and the days that followed have never and ever been the same. I have attended and conducted over fifty of these events. What should sound funny is I did one with both my boys. Casey was on the Worship Team, and Brady was a clergy helping men reconcile issues with life and God. And Kim conducted a separate Women's Walk. These occurrences have just got to have you scratching your head, wondering if I am just lying. The whole Clark family got immersed in change. As I have eluded to in the story, it took some time. If you are still looking for that Silver Bullet? Just stop.

There are many opportunities to have a life change. It happened to be this one for me. I want you to look closely at my words. They reflect rebellion, sarcasm, disbelief, hurt, and probably some anxiety. These were my battles that finally climaxed. My only point is that yours will also.

I found out I had missed a lot in growing in the church. I remember on the very last talk of the event, and the speaker said this: "You have changed, but you are going back home, and the things will be as you left them." In Dave's terms, that meant I just had the most significant change in my adult life, which will "fix my family." I remember going home full of spunk and life, and I remember walking in the door. Kim could have cared less that I was alive. What I didn't know, that was the truth as she had seen me change a million times from being non-erratic to crazy and sane to insane. To her, this was just another one of those times. Dave was as inconsistent as one might be in life. She quit being respectful of me for a long time. Well, Kim was dead wrong. I knew that I knew that there was no sign or signal that the Dave Clark Kim knew was the same guy who came back home. I left that Dave in a retreat center in the Texas Panhandle of Texas, and I never looked back. It was my full-time Life Changing experience. Yes, it was like those probably you heard in church life.

My continued advice is, don't "put this book down yet," but know a spiritual connection is a part of everyone's awakening to change and critical to being an effective father. There is no question all of it happens in different ways and means. And I will say very bluntly. I don't care how it happens. Take it!

So, let's talk about those "church, revival, or near life tragedies that change lives." You may have mixed messages from what you have read so far, but we might have more in common than you may think. I bet I am a lot like you. Remember, I came from an oil town in West Texas, a middle-class guy with everyday struggles just like everyone else. I am not a rich or religious guy where life was just perfect, and we all loved Jesus. I can say I had the privilege of seeing all or some of it from someone rolling in the church aisles to a Billy Graham revival salvation response. I saw what I considered a dead person come to life for no medical reason. And maybe years later, half of those events remain real, authentic, life-changing, and not just a memory with a great smile on how it felt. I am the first to say I have seen patients in ambulances, helicopters, and hospital rooms straight line on the monitor and wake up and live everyday lives. I have been on a Life Flight helicopter trip with a person with multiple cardiac defibrillations. You call them "dead" only for that heart rhythm to begin again. I can never deny the miracles of God.

You see that patient you treated years later, and they are full of life, vigor, and speak of miracles in their lives as easy as telling you how the weather will be that day. It remains a real, authentic, and present reality. Then there are those whose life changed only for a season. Do I get that? You bet. I had many seasons of ups and downs. My family had experienced many of those with me, only to have little faith that any of them would stick for life. Well, this did. It was not ever "the"

Walk to Emmaus. I want you to understand that you don't have to get on the web and find a Walk to Emmaus weekend retreat. It can happen in the middle of your living room with trusted friends who can pray over you and that you trust them just a little and maybe no more than just a little. I want to be very clear in saying with all my heart that this has nothing to do with religion, a church name, or a denomination. It is simply not any of that. If any of these has hurt you, leave that bag outside. This opportunity is about being connected with your deep yearning for the One who created you in your mother's womb. Let's call it Your Father. I knew very deeply in my heart that I was losing everything and everybody of importance. I was tired, angry, disappointed, and spiritually empty. I had to trust God for maybe the first time (in my head). It is always the head that gets in the way of the heart.

There are bookstores and the web full of stories about "the event" that changed my life forever. You hear the story about the person who claims, "I saw Jesus. He came right down here, and He hit me right between my eyes." "OMG, I got the biggest goosebumps of my life!" "It knocked me down on my butt, and I have never been the same," says the man who went to his one Easter service or revival service. Do I wait on my "big Event?" Where do I find it? Where do I go? And then there is the quiet voice lingering in the back of your mind saying but "what if nothing happens?" I will shortly address this.

The point of this discussion is your unspoken question. Are you going to risk getting scared about the spiritual stuff in the world? So, let's be real straight right here. Being a spiritual leader is a significant part of being an effective father. I did not say a church or a religious leader. I will not leave you high or dry with just a good story. Maybe you aspire for change that goes away in a few months. I will leave you with "The Seven Secrets of Effective Fathers." It will be your job description of this father deal. I promise you it fills the vacancy of your heart on fathering. As you read through the course in a few chapters, you will say, "I already have most of that down, and none of this is like Geometry (thank God)." You will be right. However, the biggest obstacle to being an effective father is linking it to the one thing I have been eluding to in every chapter – forgiveness.

It had to take something to make me change! Was it called "this or that" or some religious term or some awakening resonant episode within my life? Well, I used the phrase, "I got delivered, or sometimes I say I had a major bowel explosion or I had a major change in my life like none other."

That devil just wasn't going to have his hands on me anymore. Let's just tell him to leave in the Name of Jesus. Or, I had these deep growling voices, and hissing and eyes rolled back in my head and fell to the floor. That is a scary picture. It must be all real because it happened to me. Men ask me everywhere I travel about what happened. And I would say in raw man terms, "God just knocked me out with His power and love (and He did). Or, I would even go onto to say that I believe in instant miracles! I do believe in the instant miracle of God because I have witnessed miracles all over the world. Despite what I know about health and the body and the spirit within the body, I can never deny the reality of a miracle. I have seen things with people in Africa that had no explanation, but it happened. The way I explained it depended on the person who sat in front of me and the best way they could understand what I meant. We all have different pictures associated with words. Don't get hung up on an inadequate explanation of what happened but the reality of the experience.

I have told the story of how my life changed in that retreat center hundreds of times worldwide. Years later, a pastor in that same weekend event with me was the one who asked me if I was willing to continue my life of hurt or not?" He had heard my story dozens of times years after that weekend. Years later, he asked me one question. He said, "Dave, there is no question. I know your life changed forever that evening in 1996. I was there with you, but I have one question for you." Man, I was all over that and said, "sure, and you bet, and what is the question?" With a simple question and assuring and supporting smile, he asked, "How long did it take you to finally say Yes?" He wasn't questioning the reality of instant healing we hear about all over the media or my experience. He was simply asking me a great question about what caused your change? It was the simple "Yes," which meant to me in my deepest soul that I was tired and full of despair. I said Yes to letting it go. And simply said, "God was God." How God moves and works is different for each of us. So, I have a word of advice. Don't get caught up in the nuances of Christian stories about rolling on the ground and all that. I have seen them worldwide and been a part of them with different traditions from Africa to Pakistan churches. My wife can tell you I can be critical (and cynical) about some conversion stories. You must ask the question: "Does that matter for me?" My answer is almost the same every time. No. Go dance, scream, roll in the dirt, or kiss the carpet in my living room. Each of us experiences God the way He intended for each of us. He knows me the best. Don't let a church or so-called Christian dictate how you receive the Father or maybe hurt you in the past. They may be the one that needs some kind of healing and change.

So, it bears the question from me to you, "have you gone far enough with those battered or fractured relationships to finally saying Yes? Is it time to let go of the little boy's hurts of being hurt, disappointed, abandoned, and angry?" And you know, the same goes for your wife and all women because the father relationship is about little boys and girls. Little girls cannot grow up and be effective mothers without walking away from the hurtful past that defines our lives and actions through a father relationship or lack of one. We can't be healthy parents or a husband-wife team without each of us making that journey.

You noted I had said little about a church but only an experience I had with God, the Father. I never denied the reality of God. I will admit all day long that some of it seemed very real. It was in my head, my childhood, adulthood, and consumed much of my life. In all of that, I had to admit that this Jesus guy sometimes just felt like Jesus's picture in the church hallway or a story called the Bible, and Christmas was all about His birth. God seemed to be the Greater of Great that blew any imaginative thought to bits. How do you get your heads wrapped around God? Pretty awful, huh? Maybe I will surprise you when I say it was nobody's fault.

I sat in church for many years, where the reality seemed academic without emotion or much else. It was more about how I grew up. No one was at fault, including me. The truth is I had missed it. It seems when you pile up all your anger, disappointment, or a fractured family relationship, it simply didn't have a reference point. There was something greater than all of that, and "it was always there." But it didn't seem to connect with my deeper senses emotionally. I realized anger had no place to go but toward someone else. It was all wrong. My background in life says someone had to be at fault. It had to be the church or that pastor or youth pastor, and all of that is simply not true – maybe we should call that a bad deflection from the real truth.

So, whatever words of explanation we try to use, let it be you. Whether it sounds a bit religious-like "deliverance," or I had goose-bumps, or I felt like I fainted or felt a warm and rushing feeling all over my body, use the words best for you. It doesn't matter what anyone thinks about any of this. The only reality is one day, you said a deep and inner Yes to the greater. In the protestant religions, we call God, The Father, Supreme Being, and the list goes on. We will talk more about all this. So, don't derail on me with the Yes but be ready for the Yes.

Chapter 14
Life after Jail

As you might remember, in the early part of the book, I mentioned bits and pieces of my story might sound like parts of your life. I spent a lot of time talking about my story, intentionally trying to be personal and intimate about my life. I think it's about those small or large parts that bind many of us to the same issues of family, fathering, and the importance of our childhood, teen, and adult lives. For many years I felt I was a man on an island that seemed different than most. I thought that no one would understand issues in my life or my childhood and my family. I felt no one would understand I had to work and be successful, or this life would evaporate with a failed job or even the loss of a job. I felt no one would understand the guilt feelings I had growing up with my health. I felt no one would understand how big personal and family performance played such a big role. As I talk to men across the world, I hear hundreds of Dave's stories. I listen to things like, "Dave, you don't understand that if I lose my job, my family will have no one to turn to for help. My wife will take the kids and go live with her folks." Dave, "I work all the time. I have no life, energy, or time to go home and be the model husband and father because I am exhausted and working on fumes."

If nothing else, if you are continuing reading with me, I would guess you have determined we have something in common. I bet I understand your relationship with life, family, marriage, and being a father if your life somewhat resembles just a part of my story. If you remember, I spent a lot of time talking about my childhood, college, and life with my older son and the effect it had on my family. All of us have different stories, but they are remarkably the same in emotions' fundamental issues. So, don't get hung up on Brady and me. Your story may be about a daughter who got pregnant or ran off with an older man or was addicted to drugs. Every one of those stories will have a connection to my outcome. It is when I said the word, Yes. I am not using the word, Yes, to dedicating your life to Jesus or joining a church or any of the church rituals. Don't go there. I am saying Yes for The Father to help me, guide me, being ever-present in my loneliness and hurt. I am saying Yes for the Father to be real to me. So, let's say this right off. You will have to trust me when you let that happen that He tends to take care of the rest. I don't want you to be surprised or disappointed when I say Nothing came quickly. I didn't wake up with my marriage improving, or I was suddenly the dad out throwing catch with his son at the park. Nope.

As you will read a bit later from my wife, Kim, it took years for my wife to trust me again. I can probably say something similar about things she did to hurt me. But this is not a tit-for-tat deal. As I said earlier, you might have hoped there is a Silver Bullet for a quick fix. What took years to form and develop in our lives just does not go away – sorry. If this is disappointing, I am sorry. I did feel that way. I was all about doing it and fixing it. Finally, I figured out what went wrong and what I needed to do right for my family. When I was ready, they were done. It took some time because when you have a wife and husband hurling boulders at each other, you must break that boulder down into small stones and pebbles. Only then do they have a chance of washing away. Unfortunately, time is a factor in healing and restoration.

Saying "forgive" me takes substance behind saying it. You have to be careful in using the words "I am sorry" because we use them in such slang and freelance mannerisms. I think wives and husbands don't often hear the words, "Please forgive me," and when you do, it does get a different response. There are not a lot of similarities between being sorry versus forgiveness. Those two actions are wide apart as oceans dividing continents. You can get on a whirlwind of book references on the difference of the words. For my purpose, I am not really dealing with the superficiality of being sorry. In dealing with fathering wounds, it has to get deeper.

Still, it all comes down to a simple fact: Forgiveness deals with the heart. Forgiveness is not necessarily letting anyone off the hook.

Now, a lot more is written on forgiveness, so if I have struck a few nerves with you, take it on your own to further dive into this subject. Saying I am sorry doesn't reach the depth of emotion in saying, Will you forgive me? Let's look at it in these terms: "Kim, I'm sorry for flirting with my secretary at work and lying to you about my feelings toward her. When you confronted me about it in the car, I just blurted out that you don't ever show me love. I said it to hurt you because I have needed more from you lately. Will you forgive me? There is a big difference between that and "I'm sorry for what I said." Let me take that one more level from forgiveness. Do you really think that wife is ever going to forget that her husband had been flirting with his secretary every time she sees the secretary or hears her name? Probably not. Forgiveness is linked to trust, and usually, a forgiving act attaches itself to some violation of trust. Be clear. This stuff is not just about writing a letter or blurting out a "Please forgive me" and walk away, calling it finished. Let me assure you. It is not complete with a check on your check-off list with your dad, child, or wife.

So, Can You Risk a Bit More of a Read?

To his credit, Brady flew through probation with flying colors. As Brady changed and became isolated from bad friends and influences, he experienced healthier life choices. Ironically, he went to work as an Assistant Youth Pastor after rehab and spent the first summer in a Christian youth camp. Later, I would get a call about Brady at the church camp. I held my breath as though time had stopped. To my surprise, they would say that Brady has the most charismatic and life-changing influence on the youth at the camp. They went on to say that dozens of kids were experiencing life-changing decisions every day. My first reaction was that an alien from outer space had jumped into his body. They had to be talking about the wrong kid. Let me put a small grin on your face right here. The fact of the matter is that Brady went on to a four-year Bible college. That was a miracle with his grades. Hold on, he became an All-American soccer player, graduated, and began his ministry in Dallas, Texas, with World Impact. This ministry was committed to home church planting in at-risk population areas. His ministry was in a gang-ridden and high-poverty area in one of the largest cities in Texas. It seemed Brady went to outer space and came back in a different body. Today, Brady is a profound and powerful pastor with a passion for the poor and is a great father.

The scripture of "the least of these" expresses the heart of Brady. He is a recognized community and faith leader. Funny, they say, "Just call Brady Clark. He will get it done." Recognize that statement earlier in the book? OK, I will refrain from all the religious words to say it was a miracle from God. Brady got delivered from the Devil. God reached down and changed Brady Clark. Praise God! Well, I will say in very simple words, Brady said Yes to the Father and let go of years of pain and hurt and failure. God did the rest. Did magic occur between him and me or our family? The quick answer is No.

Casey had his own story going. His high school journey involved being successful with theater, student council, music, good grades, and great friends. To this day, people love him for his acceptance of people and a personality full of understanding, passion, and being authentic. He took a lot after his mother with good grades and her personality traits of kindness and thoughtfulness. Casey is a deep thinker with a balanced worldview on his opinions and philosophies. He went on to college with a detour of going to sound engineering school and working in the audio-video field before finishing college with a major in international studies and a minor in Russian. After pursuing a career in the music industry, he entered a second career path in the healthcare field, which is pretty amazing. As my dad and me, Casey worked with me on rural health issues, analytical writing, and research. He is brilliant and intuitive.

You have to ask yourself how the little brother or little sister fairs in such a toxic environment. Casey could write a book about being the good kid in the wrong place. I hope he writes his book for the thousands of brothers and sisters who were victims in a toxic environment. I think while trying to hold a family together and perhaps rebuild one came shortfalls. There was a lot of attention swinging to Casey. Still, in reality, it was more about damage control than anything else. It seemed more about seeing Casey happy. There is one flaw in looking for a smile. You have to be looking for what the smile is masking in hurt. As I figured out much later in life, "Little Dave" had bundled up a lot of anger, disappointments, and hurts that I didn't find healthy ways to deal with all of them. The key is how "big Dave" assures that "little Casey and little Brady" is not my age trying to work through childhood issues. In this cycle, you become depressed, overwhelmed, feelings of failure, lack of female commitments, and I don't see a future in all of this. That wasn't far from how Casey felt. Then came the opportunity to move to Amarillo for a new career (funny, huh?). Things changed. In the meantime, the feelings with a sense of failure are prominent behind his mask. As Casey might say, I lost my voice in the midst of all of it. The interesting issue with me is my missing helping Casey pursuing his voice. When dads wear masks, kids learn to wear masks, and we all get used to seeing each other with masks hiding the real person. It becomes a crippling emotion.

The point of this is to say it may be about one of your kids, but the others can be as big of victims as the one requiring all your attention. I think you can just count on that reality.

Fathering is on Us.

It was during this time that I had a huge question I had to answer. How was I going to maneuver through all the pain, disappointments, disagreements? And what might be concluded just being a failure of raising an older son whose risk for death, prison, or failures with marriages, drugs, and relationships were sky-high? My wife, Kim, had been experiencing depression. In Kim's words, she would tell you she was pretty done with God and Dave. She will tell you that she cried out to God every day. When Dave walked away from the church, she felt the responsibility to be the spiritual leader. After a long time, it seemed that the "well came up empty," so crying and pleading to God, she concluded, "I am done with all of this." Her anger toward herself and me was toxic and destructive, which further hurt our marriage and herself. You see, you can't hear clearly when you are full of hurt, pain, and being depressed. During our family crisis, Kim finished her accounting degree and CPA certification at a local university. She was a successful financial comptroller and accounting director for a large grocery firm. Work filled the hurt and disappointments of a failing marriage and family. So, as you watch one son play for a national soccer college championship with a new mind and body, and the other is at an acclaimed university, there sits a fractured marriage. Wow, God, I thought when Brady got fixed, it would be all ok. The happy family moves on – wow, thanks a lot. I missed that one.

So, guys, this is where some things in the story might get a bit murky if you are either mad at God or didn't much like Him in the first place or maybe disconnected like me. It probably really doesn't matter. It all rests in your court. The question is the same as what do you do about it?

I want to leave you with this thought before I forget it. This family and the fathering thing falls on you as the father. You must get things resolved, or things will tumble around you. Your wife and kids will find other means of survival when it becomes obvious you may not be willing to deal with the hard answers that are required. If you want this thing to work, it requires resolving the challenging problems. I keep saying to you not to get hung up just in my story. Where are you in your personal story? As you read along with my stories, what experiences as a little boy or teenager, or college kid is popping up that helped form you as a father and husband? What are your work ethics? Do you have intimate relationships with your kids? Are you and God talking? What legacies of your family are affecting yours? Are you and your wife really and truly madly in love with each other – really connected in all aspects of life? What are your fears? What parts of work or life are discouraging? Can you sense you are depressed or seemingly up and down on any given day or hour? Are you quick to anger? Hey, let's stop there. Enough is enough. I have opened myself up by giving you my laundry list I had to answer, and I took one at a time. Maybe you need to sit and answer these questions and others that pop up. How do some of them fit with your story? In a sense, the book is a lot about your self-examination as a father and husband using my life experiences to help jog your memories or experiences.

Earlier, we talked about why you picked up this book. Perhaps you hoped there were Ten Best Solutions to be a Better Dad or Husband (again)? You might have thought your marriage is now alive (again)?

Maybe you visualize both of you walking down the beach barefooted, holding hands looking at the sunset? You look like a Hallmark card. Your hair is blowing in the wind, and you even have on matching white shirts with great tans. Wow, I like that look. I will come back to this image later in the book, so don't think I am making fun of that image if I just described you.

You had the opportunity to throw the book in the trash when I stated upfront there is no Silver Bullet. When I say, "Sorry, it is not that way," don't throw this in the trash and say, "See, you're like everyone else with no real answers." Hold on. I do have answers which men testify all over the world has changed the very fragment of their lives and family. You have to realize one thing. I would never take the risk of writing something that was not totally on target and dead right. Being a retired guy on a fixed income and not having any reason to spend three years on something I have never done or had to do should be reason enough. I would not be writing a book like this if it were 100% right.

Back to the Tumultuous Years.

As Brady was in his rehabilitation program, Casey was finishing high school. I was relieved in many ways. For one, when Brady was in jail, we knew where he was and that he was relatively safe. Brady entered the rehabilitation program in the same town where we lived. Again, we knew he was safe. Brady only went to rehabilitation and completed it (in his words) "not because of my dad, but my mom." It did bring relief to our home with our younger son while we got our days back to a stable schedule. Before, we felt like we were only a phone call away from the local hospital emergency room or police. Remarkably, Casey was doing well in high school. It seemed some things were beginning to get a better rhythm. Here is what I missed in thinking everything is going to be OK. There is that wreck down the road that has been waiting for you. It is going to require action by you one way or another. If you ignore it or those hidden wounds of your family trauma, you will create generations of dysfunctional kids and families. It will get you.

Through all of this, Kim and I never saw eye to eye. She came from a more passive personality, and I was from an "in your face" personality with little compromise. I knew that Brady had to pay for all he had done. I will admit that it made me vomit. Amid the tough love talk, no one tells you about how you can't keep food consumed or numerous sleepless nights and workdays are a blur. There are nights of poor communication among everyone in the family. To say you are living in a minefield is an understatement. This whole tough love idea is tough! We talk with families across the world. They tell us their son or daughter is in jail, and what do they do? Our response is almost always the same – leave them there. Is there a worry? Yes. We will also say a few more clarifying statements.

We had local friends who were judges and worked in law enforcement. Once when we knew what jail they had placed Brady in, we called a judge friend. His advice was to leave him because he was in a good jail and should be fine. He gave us good advice to try and determine if a jail had a good or bad reputation. He advised us if the jail had a bad reputation for bailing him out on a bail bond.

My advice for the father and mother is unless jail was truly a life-changing event in their life, you might want to leave them in jail when the second time occurs. I hate to sound negative, but statistically, it will happen. The reality is that kids need to pay for what they did to others and the impact on your family. Life has consequences, and parents need to be firm. Moms and dads need to see eye to eye as the kid will play every family member against one another. Just brace yourself for things you never knew about your kid. We used to say that when Brady was moving his mouth, he was lying. You hate to say or think those things when your kids lied and stole from you. Kids are smarter and more manipulative than I ever imagined from my days growing up.

I decided early into our home crisis that I needed to be straight-up with the President of our hospital. I was a Senior Vice-President with high standards of performance and responsibilities. The last thing I needed was to lose my job. I ended up in that large Baptist Hospital I described at the red light driving into town that late-night from El Paso, Texas. I was a key player in critical programs without room for failure. So, I had a closed-door meeting to explain our unfolding family tragedy with my boss, the hospital president. I left with his promise that if my job performance was sliding that he would let me know so I could correct it. Why? My child and adult personality said, "Dave, you can't lose your job and everything in life." You have to be not only on your best but your very best." Guess what? I became obsessed with job performance and long hours because my childhood insecurities came screaming at me even though I was in a highly secure position. My child's insecurity screamed at me, going home from work. The voices were the same as not being good enough. The voices kept saying I needed to do better and not let anything go undone. Yep, it drove me further being a workaholic and away from being intimate with anyone in my family. In the midst of this, I went back to school. Finally, I finished that bachelor's degree that I walked away from in El Paso with a Healthcare Administration degree. In the midst of this, I failed to see all the red lights of Kim's pain and our relationship.

We went to church. That is about as good as it gets. We both sat sort of numb in the balcony of the church Sunday by Sunday, hoping not to speak or interact with anyone. We both knew the importance of being in church in times of crisis, but we were so deep in dismay, we could barely get dressed and drive to church. I knew from my family's background in ministry; it might be fruitful to meet with the church's pastor. Despite me fighting my elite position at the hospital and my name in the community, I found myself fighting back pride to go and tell our story. But I made an appointment and found myself sitting in the pastor's office. As we greeted each other, I found myself telling the story before he stopped me midway through the meeting. He just looked at me and said, "Dave, this is not what I do." Well, I had to stop a million thoughts going through my head. To my thinking, I heard him say he couldn't really help me. What? A pastor was saying he couldn't help me. I remember walking out his door past his secretary, and she looked in shock at the conversation she overheard. I think she was embarrassed for me. I sat in my car in the church parking lot in disbelief and probably some embarrassment. I mean, I finally broke down and went into my church to be told I don't do that. Ask me if I went back to that church or any church for a long time after that incident. The answer was NO.

So, let me add on another incident that occurred with that same church and its youth pastor. Ironically while Brady was in jail, he asked to see the Youth Pastor. In both attempts, they were bitter failures with the response, "I don't do that." I remember seeing the youth pastor at a park with his new baby and wife walking, and I started making a direct trail to him. I was going to give him my opinion. To his well-being in life, Kim chased after me stopping me before I got to him. To be honest, and much later in Brady's life, the Youth Pastor confronted me in a church hallway. He asked for forgiveness as he said he made a major mistake in not meeting Brady in jail. What was sort of odd about that was I was back in that same church years later teaching a fatherhood course to college students. He saw me in the back stairs of the church, going to the fatherhood class. I told him he needed to seek out Brady for his failure to respond to him in jail. To his credit, he made it right and turned several years of bitterness for me into a better ending. It was years later that I was a keynote speaker at a regional Baptist Pastor's Convention to give my testimony about Brady and how the church failed us. The theme of the meeting was the ever-changing roles of church pastors. Several pastors had heard our talks at fatherhood conferences and felt it was a good topic for pastors to hear. Well, I didn't miss a word, pleasant and professional. "As I turned to walk away from the speaker's podium, I noticed the pastor I had approached standing in the choir." We have never seen each other again.

So, what is the point of this conversation and mentioning it in the story. Remember I said, over six people in our families are in ministry. I, better than most people, should know what some pastors do better than others and have the proper training to counsel members in life's circumstances. In bitterness, hurt, anger, and misguided emotions, we sometimes have high expectations of people we think can help us. In my case, I expected my local pastor to help me. The fact of the matter is that he was probably truthful. He didn't have the proper training to advise me through my crisis. My appropriate approach was to probably seek out a trained counselor who could not only hear my story but navigate me in my crisis. I left his church, never to return. That was not on the church but me. Be smart about seeking out the right resources in your community. I blamed the church and anybody else I perceived who couldn't help me. The fact of the matter is I didn't seek advice from other professionals because I was too proud. Still, I placed an unrealistic expectation on someone I thought should help me. The fact of the matter is most pastors lack the training in clinical pastoral counseling. Just stick that in your briefcase for future references.

All this is to say that I let people (and my anger) drive me further from the church. I was a Baptist Hospital Senior Vice-President going to a Baptist Church and an involved community leader. I was not going to trust one church member with our tragedy, and I didn't. The reality of the matter is making sense sometimes doesn't make sense. Brady and I were featured in a local magazine article on our family story a short time after we reconciled our issues with each other. Many church members saw the article and called to say they never knew what happened in our family and why we didn't share it. We did go later to share our story, but part of the story was that we did not trust people with our hurt. Hear me clearly when I say that not trusting friends with your pain is not allowing friends or family to help. I was on an island, and I counted only on myself, not anyone else. I am here to say that it was a flawed belief because some of our best friends today loved us through this time of our lives. You fall into a time of shame, hurt, anger, disappointment, and utter disbelief. These descriptions pretty well hit the middle of the target for our family.

Of all the years of pain, failure, reading every book and self-help book on the planet, I had missed the simplicity of saying Yes. Was it magic of all magic, the miracle of all miracles, as we might say? No. I came home the third day of this men's weekend retreat to an angry and sad wife who could have cared less about any experience. Why? She felt she had said Yes, several times. She will tell you that she felt God left her and did nothing to answer her pleas for her family. Little did I know in the years of strife and hurt, she had drifted further into her despair, depression, and her love for me. Kim had seen me change, try to change, and be better when I was inconsistent in my behavior. As bad as I wanted to be, things just kept tearing me apart from the guy she dreamed of the day we said Yes in the marriage chapel. It was good a lot of the time. Our marriage's reality was me not seeing how this horrible family tragedy drove Kim to her own dark world that she would later regret. I had to face the ugly part of my failures despite my desire to be a wonderful man, husband, father, provider, helpmate, lover, and all the beautiful descriptions of her dream man. It seemed to fade away.

Her feelings with Dave's "This Time" was whether it was just going to be another "This Time?" Give Dave some time. It will all be the same. He will be on fire and throw water on himself at the same time. What happened? As I have painted my picture of myself up to this chapter, my life had a lot going on. I dare say my life was not much different from your life growing up, high school, college, work, family with some extra twists here and there. If you are a dad experiencing a Prodigal Son or Daughter, as I said at the first of the book, we might be amazingly the same. Of all my experiences before that weekend and me sitting in that chapel is that "I got that God is big enough to forgive Dave and Dave can forgive Dave and God can love Dave and Dave can love Dave." It was always simple. But my beliefs, my old psychological and emotional formations of thinking, habits, family traditions, hurts, joys, and life experiences got in my way. I had some missing pieces and malformed behavior. As I sat there, and if you are honest right now, some of your parts may not be fitting well. It may not be on the spiritual side like some of mine. It is evident in my story that I had some missing parts in my idea of fatherhood.

I was inconsistent, had some anger issues, probably not too much different than most. Maybe? I had a very demanding job that still might not make me special. The true reality of me standing at my own house after my weekend experience, with my weekend bag in my hand and my friend driving off, leaving me there was I Knew a New Guy was at the door. Kim had no reason to believe it or trust that. I later realized that it would take years for Kim to forgive me, Dave forgive Kim and Brady forgive Dad, and Dad forgives Brady. And Casey had to forgive all of us. Then I had to learn a different way to love Casey, and he trusts that Dad was authentic and real and trustworthy. Casey had learned well to get into a safe place. It reminds me of my behavior of running down the hallway to my room and pretend I was asleep to avoid the wrath of my dad. It would take time for trust to be re-established. You find yourself fighting the inner voices remembering words, conversations, and flashbacks. Casey would see himself quietly hide and maneuver around the conflicts.

Maybe you may think a weekend kumbaya and some gut-wrenching talks will solve father issues? Let me say with great love and confidence that you may have just opened a deeper cavern of issues. Trust me in saying a two-day retreat may only pierce the past years of conflicts. It will not solve many of your concerns in the long term without a short-term and long-term plan. That retreat is unlikely to solve many long-term issues on your own. It may only mean you are having the opportunity of discovering your willingness to pursue the past. If that is the only resolve of the retreat, you now have more than you ever anticipated.

Take it for sure. Rejoice in that you feel hope. However, it is doubtful that you will get in your car and walk into your house, and everything will be great. You may view it as that awakening and your determination to fight for a family. You might remember that she and the kids haven't changed from the times you wish had never occurred, but they did. My point is that a one-weekend retreat or whatever event will not change years of behavior and mistrust. I was excited. I loved my wife despite some ugly things, I loved my kids despite some ugly stuff, and they could love me, and I loved me despite some ugly stuff. We had lots of beauty to hang onto and never forget that. I have talked a lot about hurt, anger, pain, and other raw emotions. I need you to now realize you are identifying your enemy as well as your beautiful experiences. These beautiful experiences desire more. When you have cut off and pruned the dead and ugly stems, then all of you can experience a new beauty and love. So, amid this fathering issue is reconciliation and forgiveness. If forgiveness is not a great word for you, then try using "forgiving a debt."

There is one added note to the story. I came to the realization my priorities were all messed up. Like my dad, life centered on work. I came to the reality I had to make a change. During this time, our hospital was going through consolidation with a Catholic hospital. While I made the internal and emotional decision that I needed to quit my job and make a life change, there was no way. However, toward the end of this consolidation, my boss, the hospital president, called me to his office. He told me I was in an excellent place for a new position for this "new hospital." But, not knowing the future or trusting the future, he offered me a two-year contract with full benefits if I wanted to step out. He, better than anyone, knew my story.

After our time of going over the good and bad of the new hospital consolidation, I accepted the contract. Here I sat looking at the brightest day of my career, thinking about how I had worked my butt off for this one moment of promotion. I knew I had to save myself and my family, but until that meeting, I didn't have the means to quit my job and not have any income. I found myself looking for a door out, and he just gave it. After a few months of lining up people for their future roles, I took a two-year leave from work. Dave was the Number One priority in my headlights and how to restore my family. After that and 20 years of my own successful healthcare consulting business, I retired at 71 as a successful hospital consultant. The difference is that I had better control of myself and my life and, subsequently, my family. Work was beginning to find it was further down the list of priorities.

It was during this time that I found myself involved with the National Center for Fathering. I became a national fathering trainer after buckets of crying, forgiving myself and others. It became what is now a twenty-year fathering ministry across the globe. Even for me, it is an amazing story. I still get off the plane in Pakistan or Africa and pinch myself if this is really happening. How could this ugly and embarrassing story be so important? I have the opportunity to share with men this story, which isn't all about Dave's shame, hurt, anger, and a family tragedy. It is how to get out of your bad places and get positioned for being an effective father and husband, grandfather, brother, and friend. It was not about the story but how we find this forgiveness and transformation that begins a new hope.

You may think I am picking on you or your father, but it is about us. We stand at the head or center of our family as a provider, protector, spiritual leader, and champion. I have been the first to stand in front of Presidents of countries, government leaders, men, women, kids, pastors, and say one profound thing: "I was not a good dad, but I found my way and here is how." You can tell by the length of this story that it takes but a minute to be changed but followed by years of a new discipline. I found we can be transforming into who we are and our relationships with our kids and their mother. The keywords in the prior statement are "years of a new discipline."

Chapter 15
Kim's Chapter

I hope you take a moment for a quick break and settle in for the remainder of the book.

This chapter is for the end of the story, for you to hear Kim's perspective of her home and family. It is not just about this one chapter because we share these stories worldwide. As I have been the primary author, Kim and I both share all the stories on stage as one. I share from my side, and Kim shares from her perspective. We want men always to remember this fathering thing is just as much about her because parenting takes a team.

From Dave: This story is as much about Kim dealing with a bad kid and me as anything else. Kim could write her own story to women about how you stay married to a man like me. She has a CD available on our website (www.thefatherscry.org) titled "What Women Want." Her story is very dramatic. I would encourage you to hear a wife's perspective on her husband - Me.

We didn't begin training fathers together. It soon became a reality for me that men need to hear the perspective of a hurt mom and wife. I could talk all day about how I hurt her, but It became different when Kim told men how I hurt her. She has a powerful impact on men who may tune me out when they think there is nothing I can share about fatherhood. When she begins to talk about her hurt, you can look across an auditorium of men (and their wives) and listen at a new level. As Kim and I travel, speak, and train, we now do it as a couple when security allows.

In many cases, it is simply not safe for an American woman to travel in some parts of the world with threats of kidnapping and abductions. Pakistan denied a second VISA on a previously planned trip. On my last trip to Pakistan, Kim went with me with increased security for both of us. Her impact on Pakistani men and their wives was enormous. I will never forget her standing in front of 5000 men and women telling her story and speaking on the most prominent Christian Pakistani satellite television show. I guess you might think it would be odd for a woman to tell a man about fathering, much less in Pakistan. And it is, but Kim speaks from the perspective of a wounded wife that had to live with a man like me. Her story teaches men what a wife wants for her children, her marriage, and herself.

I think you will enjoy her part of the story.

From Kim:
Acceptance

We all want it, right? When I was sixteen, something happened to my DAD that showed me what acceptance is all about. He was the strong, silent type of guy, a real man's man who was easy-going but hard-working, liked to hunt and fish, and valued his family. What happened to my dad occurred on a Sunday morning. He was standing outside the church, smoking a cigarette before going in so no one would ask him to pray, while my mom was already inside. When Dad went into the adult Sunday School classroom, someone new was there. This guy started talking about his experience with the Father. The thing was, he was real! He talked about real stuff, like his affairs with women, his struggle to quit drinking, his bad temper, and even his lack of closeness to his kids. Something happened in this guy's life that changed him from the inside out. It touched my dad in a way that he opened to that same Spirit of the Father and found acceptance, along with love and forgiveness. Dad didn't have to get his "stuff" together because he was accepted just the way he was.

Dad became a man who exhibited that same love, acceptance, and forgiveness in a way I had never seen, and guess what? I felt accepted and cherished by him. Not that I ever felt unloved by any of my family, but this was remarkable. He went from being the strong, silent man who came home from 10-12-hour days at work to eat and sit in his chair to a strong, confident, and expressive father who interacted with our family and friends. It made an impact on our whole family.

Acceptance was a mission for me as a wife. Dave and I married less than one year after I graduated from high school. He was an outgoing, self-motivated, highly energetic personality. Dave naturally drew a lot of people to him, and I was no exception. He was my hero, and I wanted his creative, charismatic personality to rub off on me. I was getting more and more acquainted with him and met his family. I knew instinctively that Clark's were all about performance. It was all about accomplishment, being better than the next guy, and proving yourself. Conversations revolved around past accolades and achievements or how others should behave, work, speak, and conduct their lives. In fact, the hallmark of being a Clark was giving advice, often unsolicited. When it came to Dave, his father seldom talked about "David" but repeatedly gave an unrelenting narrative about Ronald's accomplishments – "big brother." In the Clark family, there was a lot said about sports and what an outstanding athlete Ron was. Stephen, the younger brother of Dave, also was potentially a football or track star. Well, as the second born and middle child in my family, I knew if I were in Dave's position, I would feel like I could never earn my dad's approval and acceptance. I doubt any of my in-laws realized what an easy read they were. But then again, I reasoned, all that boasting was probably just to make a good impression.

> *The problem of being so performance-driven is that there is a big hurdle to overcome—pride (among others).*

All of us are guilty of letting our pride keep us locked up inside. It keeps us from asking for help or admitting we don't have the answers. Heaven forbid if someone asks us to risk exposing ourselves, our weaknesses, by discussing a less-than-perfect part of ourselves. Pride also keeps us from developing deep relationships. We will go just so far; then, we tend to keep others at bay. One of the giveaways is when we over-react to a rather benign confrontation or perceive a question as an attack. It reveals our true insecurities.

As somewhat of a perfectionist and an extreme people-pleaser, instead of boasting about myself like I perceived Dave to do, my insecurities took me the other direction. No question, I eagerly revealed my accomplishments to my parents for their approval. But around others, I hid behind a kind smile or encouraging word, never wanting to appear better than anyone else. I knew I was no better. I convinced myself at an early age that it was better to keep my mouth shut than risk harsh correction or ridicule. So, I was quiet and shy. Again, what an understatement!

Now that you know a little about the dynamics of the beginning for Dave and Kim, you get an inside look at how we ended up doing life together as a young couple. We married on January 4th, and two months later, I turned 19 years old. A couple of weeks before our marriage, Dave turned 26. Wow! What a catch for me! An older man who already had a stable job and was starting a new career. I had no clue how scary this might be for him. He had high standards and was successful in all he did. He was not afraid of anything. He was compassionate, caring, served others, and was confident in his own identity. I had no identity yet but instead went along with whatever one might suggest. Based on expectations, I could be whoever or whatever I needed to be. I honestly had few strong opinions of my own, rarely felt anger toward anyone (except myself and maybe my brothers), and I did not use the "N" word – you know, the word NO. Growing up, I was a parent's dream and a "teacher's pet." Up to this point in my life, those traits served me rather well as far as success goes; but things were about to change. Compliance and people-pleasing were not going to work in the real world, and Dave Clark was a 'real world' sort of guy. It took a few years for that to sink in.

In retrospect, Dave and I had somewhat of a parent/child relationship. He tends to carry an air of authority about him without even realizing it. And sweet little passive Kim needed that direction. A couple of years earlier, before Dave and I even knew each other, I prayed for God to help me be the person He created me to be. I knew she was in there somewhere. As a result, I had a firm conviction: everything that happened in my life from that point on was in response to that prayer. That resolve kept me committed to the good, the bad, and the ugly. At the same time, these dynamics put undue stress on Dave. Although I tried everything, I knew to support him. I just didn't know what I didn't know. He needed a break from being in charge. He needed a way to decompress after working day after day with death, trauma, and pain.

Our children came along, and I was truly joyful. Two boys! I grew up with two brothers, Dave grew up with two brothers, and our family felt complete. Oh, there were conversations about how to raise our children (putting it mildly). From the time our first son was a toddler and tried to put his plastic toy in a light socket, these 'conversations' got very intense. There was no apparent threat to his safety because we were right there, but there could have been. I didn't realize that Dave witnessed the consequences of tragic accidents involving little ones, just like our son. Brady got the wrath of his father for the first time, not quite understanding what was wrong. I saw an intense overreaction I had never seen before. Little did I know that was only the beginning. God knew that.

I have read about children of alcoholics. I felt like I married one. When Dave was in a good place, he was very good. When he was in a bad place, it was very bad for everyone within the walls of our home. The boys and I never knew who would walk in the door from day to day or what time of day or night that might be, so we always tried to prepare. And we developed our own methods of coping. Being in a constant state of stress took its toll on us. God knew that.

As Brady got older, it seemed he quit caring which Dave was coming home. But the truth was, he cared very much. He was sensitive and compassionate like his Dad. I prayed for many years that (somehow) God would protect the hearts of my little boys from the horror of it all. I was completely ineffective in my attempt to do so. It was my job, and I failed. It was as if I was just one more child sitting obediently after trying to intervene but being told to keep my mouth shut. These were one-way conversations that often lasted an hour or more. Casey was just like me – always wanting to please. He listened to his older brother get yelled at and screamed at, belittled and berated, saw things thrown across the room, broken. There was a lot of brokenness. God knew that.

What did I do as a mother? My approach to repairing that which needs repair is to be pragmatic and level-headed. Just fix it, right? How could this be any different? I may retreat to get my thoughts together, but I seldom act out on feelings or intuition. In the case of our dysfunctional family, there had to be a reason for Dave's inconsistency. Regardless of the reason, I usually over-compensated to soften such harshness and often made excuses for the erratic behavior. I compensated by being nurturing, which is what moms do. I read to my children every night, said prayers, established routines. I helped with homework and sports, played catch, encouraged, etc. To make sure the boys always respected their father, I didn't openly criticize him. To keep them from believing that the accusations and profanity coming out of his mouth were true or real, I tried to turn their hurt and anger toward "the hospital." It was Dad saving lives and doing the work of two or three people (which he did). It was "the hospital" that made him crazy. It was okay to hate an organization because it is just a thing – not a living person. It did not occur to me that this could plant seeds of confusion when it came to work ethic and submitting to authority. Hmm. I suppose God knew that.

What else did I do as a wife and mother? I was understanding when we ended up night after night, eating cold meals. When the call came saying, "I'm on my way home." we timed everything so it would be hot and ready. Two hours later, in he came. Was I angry? No. Remember, I was not one to get angry. I was understanding. But guess what! I should have been angry!!! I consistently gave my husband a way out instead of letting him take responsibility for his actions. Over several years, I learned how to get angry and set limits to survive deep depression. God knew that.

Okay, now are you still with me? I can tell you that with many couples we speak to, this scenario happens with the roles switched. The wife reacts and is emotional, and the husband stays quiet and walks on eggshells. Often, a man will have grown up with an overbearing mother, and his wife ends up playing that role. Not good for your romantic relationship! Not only does the passion for one another wane (who wants to make love to a parent??), but it often opens the door to infidelity. A wife who plays the Mom role cannot meet her husband's sexual needs. That is often a tough conversation to have with a hurting spouse in that situation. God knows that.

When it comes to your children, regardless of age, they pick up on things said and the unspoken tension in your home. They are listening even when you don't think they are, and it affects their physical, mental, and spiritual health. Likewise, it affects their ideas of what marriage looks like, what their role, and that of their spouse, should be. You may wonder, what happened to the Clark's? You want more of the story?

A story is just that. We like to say there are two sides to every story, but that is not true. We can never know all the sides of a story. Imagine a Rubik cube. That's about how complex it gets when considering the perspective of each player in any story. And each point of view can get twisted and evolve over time. So, here is where we are at this point, according to my perspective.

- Dave is his wonderful self at work and in the community but erratic at home. He has no way to decompress and work through his grief and disappointments from the critical nature of healthcare work; thus, he hits his limit and explodes at home. Maybe like PTSD?
- Kim enables bad behavior in a sincere desire to show Dave that unconditional love can happen. She goes back to college, graduates at the top of the class, goes to work and becomes a CPA – exactly what is expected of her. She is not treated as a child anymore. But the depression eventually gets too deep for her to handle. She is about to give up because:
- Brady copes with the load he has been given – unrealistic expectations and rules without a relationship – by rebelling, easing his pain with drugs, dropping out of high school, living on the streets at 16 years old, defining himself as a Punk, and daring the world to love him. The Punk Scene represented a time of teen rebellion against the generally accepted standards in society represented in weird dress, hairstyle, and music. He had quite a following whether he realized it or not. The police were following him for sure, and he ended up in jail. God knew that, but at this point, Kim lost all hope and gave up.
- Casey, too, suffered from depression. He was a gifted musician, a good student, and an athlete, but he was also about to give up. His words in the preface of the book say far more than I ever could.

We all suffered tremendous grief. My grief was so palpable that I could find no hope whatsoever. We lost our family. We lost Brady.

It finally became evident that Dave had a very real yet treatable medical condition, affecting mood. There you go - another explanation of why Dad was a crazy man. Yet, taking his medications did not "fix" him. Yes, it helped, but that didn't change the fact that he hated his son, Brady. Those are the harshest words a mother can hear, and my respect for my husband finally vanished. I checked out emotionally and every other way I could. God knew that.

When Dave tells his story about attending a spiritual retreat where he eventually gave God all his striving and found open arms of love, acceptance, and forgiveness, he found a transformation from the inside out. If you remember what he said about the reality of God in his life, just because change occurred in him didn't mean anything had changed at home. I thought to myself, "Let's see how long this experience lasts" and "It's just another emotional high where he'll be hot one day and cold the next." But after a few weeks, the cursing didn't come back. Dave and the boys went on a trip to Colorado and didn't kill each other. Maybe there was hope. Maybe this was something real, and perhaps I could trust it. But again, Good knew that.

Above all that I have written, I want you to know there is hope. Not all families have a seemingly successful outcome (at least by some people's definition of success). In my case, however, when I let a sliver of light into the darkness of my being, it was the beginning of something that I would not trade for anything. Our marriage is what I dreamed of when we first said, "I do." With vulnerability came intense pain yet intense love for one another, and it took addressing some ugliness. You see, when hurts go unattended, hardness covers up that wound until the underlying flesh is unrecognizable. It becomes impossible to love, or so we tell ourselves. The truth is love is a choice that only the strongest, most determined person can make. Ask yourself if you are that person. Love does come back, even if it is seemingly one-sided. Reconciliation with your spouse or with a child is possible and leads to even greater joy. Never would I have imagined that Dave and I, and our two sons, would end up speaking and teaching about Fatherhood all over the world. Never would I have imagined that I would stand in front of Fathers and tell them the characteristics that all women deeply desire to see in my own children's father. These are things, along with the information Dave shares, that renew my respect and honor toward him. My list looks something like the following:

- I want him to be willing to <u>sacrifice</u> some of his interests to spend time with his kids
- I want him to <u>enjoy</u> his children
- I want my children's father to <u>exude authority</u>
- I want him to <u>respect authority</u>
- I want my children's dad to be a <u>provider</u>

I could expand on these, and I do in an article called What Do Women Want? (Available on our website). It might be a great question for parents to ask one another, not with the intent of airing grievances but of affirming and offering growth to each other and their children. Of course, as I often remind people of all ages, backgrounds, gender, and roles, it starts with you. Be the person YOU desire to be. You cannot change anyone else! It takes someone bigger than you to do that. It's about letting go and trusting that God knows and hears your cries. "Fatherscry."

It took walking through some treacherous territory, but our family began the journey to become whole and healthy. It took bravery and resolve, but there were many miracles along the way. I believe with all that is within me that the biggest miracle in one's life is the softening of one's heart. We can't do it ourselves. It takes something, no, someone bigger than us, to take a heart of stone and turn it into a heart of clay. Dave told you about our grown sons, how the rebellious son came home and now serves others, and how Casey is pursuing a career in healthcare - the very place that took away his dad. The greatest sense of pride we now have is not their accomplishments but seeing the loving, compassionate heart in each of them. It mirrors the love of the Father. Do we still have issues? Of course. But as the cloud of darkness, deception, abuse, lies, accusations, etc., lifts, we find ourselves in the best place we can imagine with transparency, trust, and light.

God knows this. God is good.
Acceptance is what he offers.

Chapter 16
The Toolbox

Let's relax from reading for a minute before we jump into some significant fathering issues. After reading Kim's chapter, maybe I need to stop and take a deep breath and relax! She always has a way of saying things that men need to hear from a woman. Earlier in the book, we discussed finding answers to our question, "How can I be an effective father?" Kim does a great job of telling you what women want. You might want to add those to your list of answers.

Kim and I have been married since 1975. You should say to yourself, "That's a damn miracle!" Obviously, it is by anyone's standards. Maybe you could learn something from me. You never want your wife to get up in front of thousands of people and talk about what she really needed from me and how her husband tore her down not only as a wife but as a woman. Again, it was the last thing I would dream of doing. But I did it. It absolutely kills me to know what I did and the years she was sad while married to me. What gives me joy is how our present marriage is intense and intimate. But boy, did it take some work. I talked about the vomit stains on my back porch over Brady. I think I spit blood for years over the reality of how I hurt Kim. I had lost touch with the "I Do" spoken that night at the Presbyterian Chapel. I saw no way of it ever being right. But forty-six years later, Kim and I were sitting in that same Presbyterian church,

The Toolbox

and guess who was preaching? Yep, you guessed it – Brady! We just laughed and cried at the same time.

I still shake my head at the irony of that picture.

You remember a few pages back my description of walking down the beach with dark tans, white shirts flowing in the wind, just like a Hallmark greeting card? You might be tempted to find a bit of sarcasm here. Well, the truth of the matter is, that was Kim, me, and our sons on a surprise birthday trip to Mexico. Kim had arranged a "re-dedication marriage ceremony." So, imagine this picture. Through the hell, our family experienced, there we were in Mexico on a beach with a beautiful sunset with our white shirts and tanned bodies. How funny is that? Who would imagine Casey was my best man, Brady was the pastor, and our daughter-in-law was the Maid of Honor. Our vows were very different from the first ones we read in that Presbyterian Chapel. It was about recommitting trust, forgiveness, renewed love, and wholeness. There is no better way to say it from a Texas boy: "It was damn emotional." Why? It was an incredible symbolic act of forgiving and renewal.

I want to take every opportunity to give you, through these stories, all the fathering tidbits I can because we never went to a fathering school. We learned to be a father from others (good and bad) relating to this fathering job. I want you at the end of the day to say to a friend, "Hey, I read this book called "The Father's Cry," and it is a good read, and you might try it. It is about what we all have in common as men and some great ideas to be effective fathers." Am I an expert? I tell folks every day, "I was a bad dad, not by design or desire. I did some things right, like teaching my kids what it is to serve. I did some things I regretted. I bet I have some tools for your fathering toolbox that will help you and your kids as they grow up." I remember when my dad died, the toolbox was the treasured item for all three brothers. We watched our dad use this same toolbox for most of our childhood and adult years. Our youngest brother has the toolbox. It remains unpainted with the same handle, dents, scratches, and many original tools that took my dad a lifetime to assemble. I am sure it is like one your dad may have in the garage. Funny, nearly all toolboxes came from Sears Roebuck. You could easily find that silver-grey box in the tool section of the store. I am hopeful I can add to your toolbox. Maybe your first need is to buy a toolbox before we talk about placing tools in it?

Trust me in saying that a simple toolbox you can carry is big enough for all that you need. It has seven tools but with those are a few attachments.

I want to take a moment to summarize some things in the book better before we deal with the toolbox. Like in every story, the story is attached to real-life encounters. At the end of the day (or life), there is a summary of stories of the little boy or teenager, young man, or father and what they meant. So, before we get into "The Seven Secrets of Effective Fathering," let me summarize a few things I spent a lot of time talking about that might have contributed to some good and bad things in my life. Like me, when I read this, what does the story really mean? Dave, why is there so much time spent in your life experiences? Let's spend just a few minutes summarizing some of my experiences in a short version. Perhaps when you open the toolbox and we start sorting tools, throwing some away, and adding some new ones that it will make better sense through the eyes of your life experiences. I often say, "It emotionally drains me to tell my story." All my stories tie to a tool that I would guess is pretty similar to your tools. It is certainly not about me vomiting out my stuff for the sake of a story. This book is more than MY story.

Let's continue.

You never want your youngest son to travel with you to Africa and watch him choke down in front of a conference full of men remembering an incident in junior high school and how much his dad hurt him. In effect, you were still watching your son in public work through his disappointments from his dad. I remember each time I watched and heard Casey talk about our relationship; I felt an auditorium full of eyes looking at me with the unspoken words of condemnation, "What a jerk." Yep, that was me. It is the most sickening feeling you can imagine. I remember Casey and I talking about how he could teach the Seven Secrets while not being married or a father. I told Casey to take each Secret and tell men these are the seven things kids want from their dads. I remember watching him talk painfully about how he saw me as inconsistent and could not trust me to do what I said, like being home on time. As you read about the Seven Secrets a bit later, imagine your son or daughter saying to you, "Dad, this is what I want you to be as my father."

So, exactly what is fatherhood? Fatherhood is defined something like this:

THE HEART OF FATHERHOOD CONSISTS IN "REVEALING AND RELIVING ON EARTH THE VERY FATHERHOOD OF GOD.

Fatherhood is inescapably spiritual – regardless of our faith background, we cannot deny it. You see, discovering fatherhood is the Divine Covenant. Fatherhood is a relationship between the Father in Heaven and you or me as fathers. You will read more about this in our course in the following pages, but did you read what I just wrote? This whole inner turmoil within Dave Clark was about the Father and me. The fighting of my church history, the experiences of my wife's family, and my own experiences were part of a battle for the Father to gain my heart. It is obvious how important it was to my life because I keep telling you about it. It came with life-changing benefits for my marriage, my sons, and my goals in life. If I didn't have a gigantic grasp of Him and me – I would never be the father I desire or you desire. I am nothing without the Father. We work all around it. We find our book of the Ten Best Traits of a Dad or whatever the name of the "how-to" books and work hard on checking off the fatherhood checklist. We believe what the world tells us about being a dad or husband. If you watch television, men are depicted as stupid, irresponsible, worthless, and just another sperm donor. But we have missed the core of fathering. I missed it. I never dug into the heart of fathering because I saw and did what generations of men commonly do without thought.

Remember I told you it took me three years to write this book. I would write, cry, gag, and laugh all in the same late hours of the night. I realized many of my stories tied to what I learned in the Seven Secrets. Remember my comment about me sitting in my fathering course and going back to the hotel room and lying on the floor just crying. It exhausted me, and I am not trying to exhaust you with this. Those three days were full of memories (good and bad) of my dad raising me. I know your dad may have tried his best. You tried many times to do your best because you did not want to fail as a father, nor did your dad. Like me on the soccer field, I simply needed to shut up when my kid missed a shot on goal or he didn't run fast enough on the field. That class time reminded me I was not building up my sons but tearing down fragile young egos. I saw the reality of me hurting them, not with a belt but with my words. As with me, my dad's words stayed with me for life. Kim reminded me when she and I would argue about our family, and I would go unhinged with my mouth, and she would always say, "Dave, words never die. Be careful what you say and to whom you direct them." Remember how fragile the hearts of our little boys and girls.

Don't you hate to pick up a book, and even halfway through it, you are still trying to make sense of it? In some of the TV shows my wife and I watch, when the ending comes, she looks at me and says, "Is that it? What did that mean? I must have missed that through the entire show. Why didn't they make that clearer?" So, I felt it might help summarize the meaning of my key experiences along the way in my fatherhood journey. Trust me. When we get to the tools in the toolbox, there will be a connection. It will feel like you finally found that socket for that wrench. It will fit and work as to the simple design of the tool.

Here we go.

Hurt and anger seemed to define a lot of my life through our family experiences. My brother and dad had a toxic relationship riddled with physical and verbal assaults. I vowed I would never raise my kids, yelling, screaming, and threatening them. But I did. It went off frequently and without warning. We saw little modeling of communicating from dad to sons.

The same went for sports, as my brother could never meet the on-field expectations of my dad yelling in the stands. I vowed never to be like my dad screaming at my sons about how they played. But I did. I vowed never to be the dad hollering at my boys in the back seat of the car about how they missed a shot on goal. My sons will tell you they wanted to jump out of the car to get away from the venom of spit and fury coming out of my mouth. The reality hit me of how I am both similar and different from my dad.

The Toolbox

Your self-image as a man and as a fully functional man is critical.

My low testosterone medical condition and low pituitary function had gone undiagnosed until after my first son was born. My doctor told me it was a miracle that I fathered a child. Throughout school, athletics, and locker rooms, this condition became a huge issue for me feeling secure in "girl and my relationships." I had many girls as friends but only a few girlfriends that I could count on one hand. In fact, I became good at keeping them on the friend level. I never moved to the romantic stage. I was small in height and less mature. Did this affect relationships with the female sex and my self-image as a man? You bet. It probably contributed to my foul mouth, pornography, and "playing out in my mind sex and relationships," as sick as that sounds and seems. I always recommend men to not only get a good physical but get their male hormone levels checked along with thyroid functions. It is generally overlooked in your physical exam because somewhere in our head is a message, we "don't talk about that." Let me just give you a piece of advice from fifty years of my life dealing with doctors and hospitals. As you sit on that exam table with your naked butt sticking to the paper on the exam table, your doctor says, you look Ok. I bet you just need to slow it down. My advice is to insist on a panel of male hormone tests. They should include at least a full battery of thyroid tests, TSH, B12, Vitamin D, a PSA (prostate blood test), and a testosterone level. There are more, but these should trigger others if necessary. Sorry, that will require a needle in your arm. If he doesn't take you up on your request, find another doctor (male or female) regardless of him being a family friend or if you have gone to him for ten years. I can hear you now, "I am not going to some damn woman for this!" Really? I have used more female doctors (just worked out that way), and I prefer them because, as odd as this sounds, they tend to understand male body dysfunctions very well. My best doctors were always female. As crazy as this sounds, some male doctors will not have discussions regarding sexual functions, energy levels, depression, etc., as many female physicians or nurse practitioners. Testosterone not only affects your male sex appetite but can be a cause of erratic mood disorders and depression. Trust me, it can save your life, marriage, and everyone involved in your life will be incredibly grateful. Either Kim or I have given me a testosterone injection every week for over 30 years. There are fewer "sticky ways," but the literature will tell you that direct muscular injection is more effective over creams or patches. Kim can tell you to the day, maybe the hour, if I seemed late giving myself "the shot." How? She will call it several things: Your moods got quieter than usual, moody, and you missed me "coming on to you for a little bedroom fun." In other words, you became very inconsistent. Oh my God, I had no idea. She had lived with my erratic, moody, and lack of consistent sexual drive for a long time. It is a great way to run your wife out of a marriage. Just don't be a chicken to talk about it. There was your free medical advice in the book.

Being raised in a successful family business would seem to be a big plus. It was for me. The message I always heard was, we had to do without, and your dad has to work hard to make us a decent living to live in a nice home. Everyone must work as hard as your dad for us to make this work. That was a huge fear of me losing my job or missing a check. If you're self-employed like I was as a consultant, it could keep you up at night. So, not only would I work my regular job, but I would also teach part-time at a local college for extra money to pay off debt. Work defined me. And like my dad, I was good, well noted, and respected. Perhaps he went a bit overboard teaching how to be a good provider and protector. Despite my motives, at least I had that Secret down to the tee.

You must work harder than the next guy. So, you must be the boss and work harder than the guy next to you to the point I would stay at work for full days with sick premature babies without any sleep. The reasoning in my head was I would be ahead or the leader of the team. I would outwork everyone to be on top. I did so at any sacrifice, not to risk being without a paycheck. There was no extra pay. My head message said that I would be at risk for my family being homeless or dependent on others. I remember my dad standing me up one day in the middle of our living room. I was about fifteen years old. He said to imagine a man on my left and a man on my right. Then he asked me if I wanted either one to be my boss or me to be the boss and have better control of work. Of course, my answer is I am going to the boss. Like all of us, whether we admit it or not, I really did seek his approval.

Fear of losing a job also meant Kim must finish college and get a job for our home, two cars, college, sports, yard, and life needs. You noted I did not include vacations because, like growing up with your own business, you worked and did not ever take off. When we married and had our two boys, we agreed that Kim would raise our sons at home and sacrifice going to college. Why? I didn't want my boys raised in a daycare center or with parents never at home. A brother was not going to raise a brother.

You must have a college degree and be the best. I have three degrees and probably would have had four if I had not quit my senior year in El Paso to pursue healthcare. Although my parents had no degree, my dad received an appointment to West Point Academy but turned it down because Mom was pregnant with my big brother. He chose his marriage and fatherhood over a military career. Why did he have to choose? He never really said anything other than knowing it was the right thing to do.

The church is the foundation of the family (God). You need to go, teach, participate, and know the rules – I missed the entire relationship with Christ. How could I be an effective spiritual leader for my children?

These are the most obvious points thus far in the story. Can you see the horrible personal tragedy unfold with a failed relationship with my first son, and that described with my dad and older brother?

Can you see me watch our younger son run for cover and hide hurt (Little Dave)?

Can you see how my family was on the brink of failure? While my older and younger brothers' first marriages failed, the reality was my "secrets" were probably worse than their marriages? Divorce was not a part of that solution – three failed Clark marriages. Not me.

Can you see how pride, ego, a drive for success, and community acknowledgment fueled my need to be more than a gas station owner? Or be a struggling middle-class family?

The stories, while embarrassing for me to write, might be similar to your characteristics that contribute to continued problems with marriage and kids. It is more than identifying your story with parts of my life. The real question I am asking you to consider is discovering them, admitting them, talking about them, and finding solutions to repair them. I hate to say this (so get ready), but most of this will probably take sitting next to that beautiful person called your wife and admitting your failures. She may try to assure you that you did a lot of good things, even if she is just nice. This effort requires forgiveness and a plan for the family to move forward. Do it as a team. Perhaps it will require a coffee or tea with your ex-wife to say some of the same things. Even with your wife or ex-wife, either might not trust a thing you say because of your past inconsistencies. Remember, it is not about her, but your need to move forward in being a renewed man, dad, and husband. The fact of the matter is your wife needs you. If you are divorced or not, your kids need both of you. You will need a relationship with your ex-wife. Don't get crazy on me when I say that. More about this later.

There is this great need for you to get back to the basics of home, family, life, and marriage and reboot your relationship. It must start with seeing and admitting some of these realities then taking the next steps of reconciliation and forgiveness. Is it risky? Sure, it is. It beats coming home one day, and the wife and kids are gone. The note on the kitchen table says, "I'm done. The kids and I have left to be at my mother's house." It beats her, saying that she fell out of love with you some years ago and found other ways to love. Those are deep and dark caverns where divorce occurs, and kids are separated from their siblings and parents. It takes more forgiveness than you will ever imagine overcoming those "fractures of marriage." I will go further to say a "broken marriage" on life-support. I was there, and believe me, the emotional drain, spiritual depletion, and psychological trauma just about put me over the edge of no hope. No one on the planet gets it better than me with how you may feel about this and all the negative voices going off in your head. You need to hear me clearly that no weekend marriage retreat will get this on track. My best advice is that you need to find yourself in a room with a trusted counselor to help you keep your head and heart in place. Suppose you don't know a counselor? My advice is to seek multiple opinions from friends or professionals you may know in healthcare. Ask a friend who can ask a friend. In time, both of you need to be sitting in the same room, working through the toughest things you may ever face. The key to this conversation is to avoid the car wreck with multiple bodies thrown across the countryside. The chances of that paramedic team or helicopter rescue team pulling you out of this are slim to none. You will never realize life as before going down that highway.

Uncomfortable discussions, but let's move on.

Friends often ask me, "Hey Clark, where is your next fathering course?" They look at me funny when I tell them Pakistan or Africa. So, it would be wrong of me to write a book and merely talk about my story with you putting down the book still trying to figure out if you are still doing the right things. So, I want you to imagine sitting with me in a conference room for two days. Imagine us in the mountains talking about the tools or what I have been referring to as "The Seven Secrets of Effective Fathers." It is one of the most acclaimed texts on fathering validated by thousands of fathers across the world. There are many good books on bookstore shelves about fatherhood. Your question should be which one works. After all, there are many stories on fatherhood written by very esteemed authors. For years people would ask me where my book on fathering was? I had to decide whether my book would look and say much the same thing other books on the market were saying about fatherhood. What would make mine different? After many years of traveling and talking to thousands of fathers, the key comment seemed to be remarkably similar, "Dave. No one talks as real and blunt about their lives as you. You are authentic and honest. You give men permission to share their deepest secrets or failures in being a husband and father. You seem to know their words before they say them." I agree. I didn't want another book full of feel-good fathering stories, but one with answers.

Who says what works? How do they know? That is the difference in the book by Ken Canfield. Ken founded the National Center for Fathering. I mentioned Ken in my book's acknowledgment about "The Seven Secrets of Effective Fathers." The book's difference is validated by thousands of men in different countries regarding the successful "secrets" to our fathering issues. I bet you didn't know that you would get a free course on fathering when you picked up this book? Every father deserves to know the secrets. I have been training men across the world for 22 years using this text. The stories from men are always real. Ironically, they all sound very similar regardless of what part of the world we teach. The same question always comes up talking with men or married couples: "how?" I tell pastors everywhere I travel that their sermon was great and touched my heart. But you failed to tell me how to do it.

It is more than head-knowledge. It is heart-knowledge, healing, and renewal that come from the very Spirit of God.

By the way, you can order the book or audio on Amazon. As some will say, I am giving you the Cliff Notes.

I hope you see some resemblance to my story and how my examples correspond with the Secrets or Tools for the toolbox. I commented earlier in the book that I went to Kansas City and sat in this same three-day fathering course at the National Center for Fathers. I remember walking to the hotel blocks away after classes and just closed the hotel room door. I can vividly remember lying on the floor, just crying. I don't think I cried more in those two days than at any time in my adult life. That would probably include either of my parent's funerals or of anybody for that matter. I remember waking up and getting dressed and walking to the course each day, still wiped out from the day before in class. It took me some time to interpret all the crying. I now know it was the years of pain, anger, and disappointment of a little boy and a man who was finding their way from my life. They had been such a part of my life that it was like a gashing, clawing, and tearing away from a person they came accustomed to living within. I don't know how to say it any differently.

My big ugly parts had no place to stay anymore. Day by day, I realized I needed to replace my pain with healthy knowledge, tools, and hope, and peace that I was afraid to touch or maybe know how to touch. Finally, a guy named Ron Nichols of the National Center of Fathering was the trainer. I sat with Ron for those days, and he had no idea he was taking a sledgehammer to my life. He didn't know I didn't have a toolbox, and he was throwing tools at me left and right. Taking a sabbatical from work, experiencing The Walk to Emmaus, and then this fatherhood experience cleaned me out and for good. I am your perfect example of doing things the tough way with resistance, excuses, and holding onto what may have been the more toxic values of my family traditions.

It became emotional for me to see my failings and internalize them. I knew I had done some things right. I became more concerned about "fixing" some things that I knew had fallen apart in me. I realized I had not done well with the material at this point and just needed to get this in my head and heart better. I will forever be indebted to Ron and how that week changed the very fabric of my life. He had no idea what was going on in this hurt heart with this guy from Texas.

Let's learn about being an Effective Father. Here is your two-day course on becoming an Effective Father. It is full of more answers. There is no need for notes as I am providing you the highlights of my teaching course. If you're not averse to writing in the book, just get a pencil out as you read. You will have the same tasks to complete as though you were in my class. This written book format was a challenge to write because I am usually in a class with men (and women) for two to three days. I promise you that you will get the meat of the material. I will "chase a few "rabbits" in some paragraphs – we do that in Texas. There are usually some great class conversations as I teach the class in person. Unfortunately, I am not able to include many of them in this book. I will attempt to address some of this as I write to give you the benefit of those comments. The bottom line, you will get the core without the fluff…. even though the fluff is many times helpful.

I want to thank you for reading up to this point in the book. Why don't you get something to drink and stretch wherever you may be sitting and let's dive into the tools or secrets we have been discussing.

OK, here we go.

Chapter 17
The Course

Day 1

The Father's Cry
"The 7 Secrets of Effective Fathers"

Thanks for continuing your reading and desire to obtain tools for your Fatherhood Toolbox we have been discussing. Thanks for hanging in here with me. For many chapters, I have been giving you answers or solutions to the questions to our fathering issues. As a result, you and I will end the book by discovering how we tackle one of the most critical issues facing you as a man. You may ask why don't you just publish these things, and men are armed with the information to be effective fathers. I believe one of the most effective ways to communicate a deep feeling is by telling life stories. I feel it sometimes takes placing ourselves in another life experience to see ourselves. I firmly believe that is why so many men won't sign up for a fathering course in their community. They never see a need even though their life is falling in pieces all around them.

When I ask ten men, do they think they need a fathering course, maybe two will say Yes? As I travel worldwide, all my friends in the states ask me why I don't teach as many courses in the states? I tell them I do, but it seems men in Africa and the Middle East have an unquenchable thirst compared to men in the United States who have more than enough to drink. How you become a better father and husband is as important today as at any other time in history.

In this first section, I hope you can visualize your struggles in being a father is very difficult in a rapidly changing world that seems very confusing. We will soon get answers that address your fatherhood concerns. These answers relate to any age or stage of being a father. Only with such information can all of us learn how to grow from other father's experiences. Obviously, I was not a perfect dad. But I have found answers with a scriptural basis regardless of your faith, well-tested, and documented with proven principles. We have discovered you can apply them to almost any faith and culture.

Let's begin with a quick overview of "What is Fatherhood" to give you a point of reference in our teaching. As we read about my fathering issues, you might have experienced a lot of similar feelings? Maybe while reading my story, you said to yourself that "I am not a bad father," or you said, "Fathering can't be all that hard; men have been doing it for centuries, haven't they?" Or, you thought, "I wished I had some time back as I made a lot of mistakes." Ha! You might have said I have no desire to be like this Clark guy who really screwed up things. Whatever you're thinking: Yes, fathering is bigger and maybe more complex than you may imagine. It is a big challenge. You see, children are unique human beings created in the image of God. They're not miniature adults. They are growing up to have their own lives, something you, as a parent, can never completely control. The world further complicates your fathering. It is even more complicated by your relationships without our fathers, many of whom were physically absent or emotionally distant. You see, we learn to father through models. Men that were raised by a single mom have large missing pieces of fatherhood principles. And there is one fact that I will just state and move on without argument, and that is that a woman can never be a father.

At the National Center for Fathering in the United States, there has been extensive study of more than 4000 fathers worldwide to determine those considered by professionals, peers, and their churches to be particularly effective fathers. These studies are by a scientifically proven Father Profile that you have access to in the book addendum.

I would like for you to review the profile at the end of the course. Men have been studied for many years. The National Center looked at their fathering practices of why these effective men had scored significantly higher than all the other dads. There are scriptures from many faith cultures that reference fathers and the fatherless. There are certain things that effective fathers do differently from all other dads. I know you may have some questions while reading the book, and I hope this chapter can further give you answers.

I want you to consider answering some questions either in your mind or writing them down in the book. Let's call it a pre-course evaluation on fathering. I would write your answers down to look back later.

Describe what you think is a Father?
What is your current relationship with your father?
Do you think you need a Father? Why?
If you do not know who was your father, who acts as your father figure?
Can your mom be your dad? Why?
What is your relationship with your mom?

Well, why is Fatherhood so Important?

THE HEART OF FATHERHOOD CONSISTS IN "REVEALING AND RELIVING ON EARTH THE VERY FATHERHOOD OF GOD."
Let's say it again.

What makes Fatherhood so important?

Fatherhood is inescapably spiritual – regardless of our faith background, we cannot deny it. Faiths of every color and nature have unique characteristics of the importance of father relationships with their children. So, fatherhood is not just a protestant issue but one for all of humankind. All little boys and girls on the planet deserve a father who holds fatherhood sacred.

Discovering Fatherhood is the Divine Covenant. Fatherhood is a relationship between the Father in Heaven and us as fathers. Right now, don't get caught up in your faith tradition or lack of faith but let's just keep focused on God. I will use the word "Father," as that is a more intimate relationship for me.

First and foremost is that a father leaves an incredible impression on his children because his role is linked to another Fatherhood. Although this other Fatherhood is unseen, every human heart has a deep, unquenchable desire to join. God has made each of us have a family bond with Him. As a result, the human heart is constantly restless until it unites the fatherhood of God.

Second, fatherhood is inescapably religious. Pope John Paul II pinpointed the heart of the role of fathers when he said that their calling is "to reveal or show and to re-live on earth the very fatherhood of God." Because fathers reflect the divine Father, earthly fathers will always influence their children to a degree far beyond reasonable expectations. As fathers, men can either greatly speed or impede their children's relationships with the Father.

Third, discovering fatherhood in the divine covenant is an intimate and personal relationship with God the Father. The Bible calls this family relationship with the Father a Covenant. The depth of God's love for us exceeds human comprehension.

To mirror the Father's love, you must first encounter the love of the Father. Being shaped by the Father's love, you can eternally shape your children's lives through family life's everyday events.

As we discussed my struggles with God, church, and relationships, Saying Yes to the Father becomes a very critical first step in moving you moving forward with establishing this divine covenant.

There are Three Important Truths about being a Father:

- Children need their Dads
- Fathering is a learned skill
- Fathering has great rewards

Before we move too much further, let's talk about the different uses of the word father, daddy, papa, or whatever terms you happen to use in your particular culture or heard growing up in your family.

I grew up with the word "dad," so my use of the word describing my father was dad. I am papa to my grandkids. Many written words are on the web about the difference between a dad or a father. Many terms maneuver into the generations of names or the meaning of these names. I am just going to be honest here, and say, "don't get caught up on some internet search engine or whatever the different agendas are out there." As you will see, the words are used back and forth in this course. We are going to focus on certain things that effective fathers do differently from all other dads. So, stay focused on this theme. You see, I am concerned about you being a father, but as much as that is, you being an Effective Father. As I read all these "word fights," I sort of just want to holler, "Hey, let's just figure out how we keep dads in families and be effective in how they father a kid. We got a bigger problem with fathers leaving their families. We have a worldwide epidemic of fatherlessness. Just shut up out there!"

Ok, short side-track. (Where I grew up in Texas, it is called "chasing a rabbit!", but it is more commonly known as "getting side-tracked with a story".)

Let's move on…

1. <u>**CHILDREN NEED THEIR DADS**</u>
   The importance of fathers is demonstrated by what occurs when fathers are not in the home.

   We find that:

   Without dads: There is an increase in school drop-out, kids suffer from poverty, the divorce rate is higher, drug/alcohol rates are higher, and there is an increase in children out of wedlock

   With dads: Kids are more empathetic; kids are compassionate as adults. The father's influence is the strongest predictor of a child's success with school and friends.

2. <u>**FATHERING IS A LEARNED SKILL**</u>
   It is not inherited. We learn from other men. However, there is a need for time to move from being apprentices to be a craftsman. Anyone can drive a nail into a piece of wood. It takes skill to

build a beautiful piece of furniture. Fathering is a process of development.

3. <u>FATHERING HAS GREAT REWARDS</u>
It is often intangible moments of success or times we can hardly define or understand. It is the moment your wife looks over at you when your son or daughter scores a point in a game with big tears running down your cheeks.

Now, let's talk a moment about how you spend your time and how that can get in your way with these three important truths. We now know that our children need us. We can get great rewards being great dads, which is a learned skill. Once you peel all the outside stuff kids may say or do, they will always tell you, "Kids need their dads."

I bet you want to be with your children more than you are, but things seem to "pull you away from this priority." You can't seem to "get a handle" on the problem. Like many, you may not be living with your children because of a marital issue or a hostile situation with your wife. Or you may be at home and find yourself still not paying attention and focusing on your need to care for your children. Or your job requires you to be out of town most of the week.

'There are four different kinds of absences. Let me describe each one. Then you determine where you fit in your priorities as a father and in which ones you can make a change.

Let's take one at a time and determine where you may be in your fathering absence. But first, let me ask you a question that just requires your inner response:

Did you have a father who was not at home a lot? For whatever reason, while you were growing up, and even today, are you absent from your relationship?

There are Four Types of Absences:
- Physical Absence
- Emotional Absence
- Psychological Absence
- Spiritual Absence

Physical Absence

Let's go back to the Introduction of the Book with a more detailed look at the Fathering Facts in the Addendum and remember some staggering facts:

- An estimated 24.7 million children (33%) live absent of their biological father.
- Of students in grades 1 through 12, 39 %(17.7 million) live in homes absent their biological fathers.
- 57.6% of black children, 31.2% of Hispanic children, and 20.7% of white children live absent their biological fathers.
- According to 72.2 % of the U.S. population, fatherlessness is the most significant family or social problem facing America. Just consider any country outside of America equally as bad.
- Among children who were part of the "post-war generation," 87.7% grew up with two biological parents who were married to each other. Today only 68.1% will spend their entire childhood in an intact family.

For us to bring this a little closer to home, this absence might include dads working out-of-town to make a living for his family. We know in Africa, the number one cause of physical absence of men is the necessity to look for work wherever work might be. The problem we have identified within Africa is that men are at high incidence not to return home and have multiple kids along the way to finding work. So, these men are creating fatherless families wherever they travel. Statistics are now showing they seldom return to the original home. This absence can also include the father, who is gone during the week and only home on the weekend. This absence is one of the greatest challenges of physical absence because generally, fatigue and continued work in a home office or being split between too many home responsibilities leave kids fatherless even if dad is present two days at home. This dad will have to work hard in being a "work away dad" with frequent calls, not missing game days, and the list is very detailed. I would refer you to our website for more articles or plans to minimize these absent failures. I encourage dads to work hard to find jobs at home whenever possible and available. I know better than most how difficult that might sound.

Emotional Absence

Although dad is physically present, he may not be supporting or affirming kids. This dad is at home but not connected emotionally. He is the dad asleep in the chair with the television remote glued to his hand or a beer sitting on the TV tray. He is not available verbally or physically to anything going on with his children. I remind dads every day to turn off their cell phones for one hour-long soccer games and be involved with your kid from getting ready for the game to get the ice cream on the way home. My kid has to know, see, and hear that they have my heart.

Psychological Absence

Psychological absence is the absence of modeling skills and the importance of the father's role. Statistics show that fatherless boys repeat the cycle of being uninvolved with their children. Let me put this in perspective: You are reclused in your home office, asleep on the couch, or you just let the wife take care of everything. You go to the mall shopping at a family outing for Christmas gifts only to walk behind your family, talking on your cell phone or texting messages.

Spiritual Absence

Spiritual Absence can be defined simply by the lack of leading by fathers in family spiritual activities.
As you read my story, you might have thought this guy was unconnected to anything but work. And you would be correct in that I was not connected Emotionally, Psychologically, or being a Spiritual Father. I was there, but as both my boys say in conferences, "dad was there," but when he was, there was a lack of connection – it was all about work." In the first hour of my fathering course, I learned

I was an Absent Father, just not how we think of it when we hear the word absence. Dad being there means connection, awareness, and commitment. Along with those are the words consistency, but we will touch on those later.

I regretfully admit the bedtime stories and nursery rhymes with our two boys always came from Kim, not me. I vividly remember having some of those great friends over to our house one evening for cards after our lives got back to "normal." It was a card game where you had to name that nursery rhyme. I quickly vanished to the kitchen after the first round to cut the pies for dessert. Kim noticed my departure and came in and asked me what was going on? I teared up with my chin at my feet, admitting to her, "I didn't know any of the bedtime rhymes." It killed me. A week later, one of our dearest friends that were present that night left a book on nursery rhymes in our mailbox with a sweet and kind note for me to have and use with my grandkids. I just sat down and wept for not being the spiritual father for my boys. Kim did an incredible job with them. I will eternally be grateful for those "eternal gems" she embedded in their hearts. While I was off flying in a life-flight helicopter or being in a small rural hospital with a premature baby gasping for air, my home was empty of a father. I believed a lie that I was doing this all for them and to keep my job. It had gone way past that irrational logic.

Here are a few questions to think about:

So, what's so hard about being a good father? What gets in your way?

Let's "Take a moment and think about the reasons that get in your way to be a good father or write them in the book. Maybe list two or three things.

Now, let's talk about why some fathering obstacles are barriers for you and why you may have difficulty in some of these issues.

Four barriers can hurt you in being a good father. I am sure there are more but let's talk about these:

1. Lack of Resources: Unlike women or mothers, men are not known for "natural abilities" instinctively knowing what to do. We generally learn from family members. When we had

our first baby, we received all kinds of baby books for my wife, illustrating how to wash diapers to recognizing a skin rash. Yep, you're right. No chapters on how to be a father. I don't remember any best-selling book on the market on how to be a father. Why? There weren't any books on how to be a father.

2. <u>Unreconciled Past With our Father:</u> This is the key barrier. I am not adding further information to this barrier because I spent a lot of time on how our past dictates our future.

3. <u>Fear of Failure:</u> Comparing yourself to your dad and saying you might not know what to do, fear of using undiscovered talents and failing to take risks. Fear of failure encompassed me.

4. <u>Lack of Knowledge:</u> Fatherhood is learned. How about a word picture: Your dad gives you a bucket of nails, a hammer, and some wood and tells you to build a treehouse. You're clueless about how to build a house in a tree, much less get up in the tree.

We know that the role of our father has a significant impact on us as men. You watched your dad while growing up and how he was as a father and perhaps watched his father. If your father was absent as a child, maybe it was an uncle, brother, or granddad that became your father mentor.

Let's chase a rabbit right here.

It is important to know how men must feel when they had no father while growing up or never knowing their biological father. He may be adopted or even a baby when his father left him and his mother. You may be that man. Even though none of these fatherhood principles change, it is difficult for a man to address fathering issues in his life, knowing that a gigantic hole exists for him. My advice for this man reading this book is to seek the same reconciliation we will discuss in a few moments.

Let me give you a word picture to view: You can view it as someone driving down the highway saying to a friend, "over there, you can see a big pasture of ugly trees and rocks where nothing will grow." Now imagine, someone came along and removed all the trees and rocks and plowed the ground, and planted new crops. We would later drive by that same pasture and say, "that use to be the ugliest pasture out there where nothing would grow but look at it now. It flourishes." The same analogy holds true for looking back at our life without a father. We can choose to see the ugly pastures we call life, and then we can forgive the past. When that occurs, we have a new view of our past, present, and our future.

Forgiveness is powerful. We discussed this earlier in the book. Forgiveness can happen even if you never physically saw that person. My family volunteers at a Youth Detention Center and has taught fathering to teenage boys and girls for years. Yes, teenagers. Why? We found over 95% of those kids never knew their dads. They had no idea of what a father is supposed to be, and the boys would soon be fathers, and girls would be marrying one. It was like the conversation with Casey and me about how you teach fatherhood when you're not married or a father. In using the Seven Secrets, we guide them to what they want in a dad, and remarkably it is a model of the Seven Secrets. So, we first walk them through forgiving that person in the form of a forgiveness letter they write to this unknown dad who abandoned them and how they must forgive them. This task is Day One of a twelve-week course. No one would dare write a letter that first week. It was not even a consideration. I remember this vivid description of a young boy tell me: Mr. Clark if you said that was my dad tied up on a tree, I would take a gun and ram it up the butt and pull the trigger. I would watch that bullet tear his insides up and blow out his brain. Then I would pour gasoline on him and lite the match. In the next twelve weeks, I watched a boy full of rage begin to become open and tender. I watched that young boy, twelve weeks later at our graduation, run and grabbed me and told me he had written his letter forgiving his dad. I think I cried all the way home. After leaving the detention center, he worked at a local grocery store as a sacker, where we shopped. That kid would leap over counters to sack my groceries and walk to the car with me. I watched a kid blossom and eventually went to college, and he had a darn good idea of how he was going to be a father.

So, let me ask the question today: How did your father impact your parenting?" Or maybe lack of a father?

The Course

Again, let's think about some things about you and your dad and maybe write those down. We will use them later.

List five ways you are similar to your dad.

List five ways that you are different from your dad.

Think about each of these and see if you can define what they may be.

For example:

- I found my dad didn't fish or hunt (remember we never took vacations). Guess what? I don't fish or hunt.
- He was a perfectionist with cars and our lawn. So am I.
- We are different in that he was good in numbers. I struggled with numbers.
- He loved to paint, and I would burn a paintbrush if I had the chance.
- He could memorize a lot, and I could barely remember a poem I was supposed to memorize.

So, you may have some positives to thank your dad for and to continue or start with your kids. And if your dad has died, then thank him in your heart through a prayer of thanksgiving. It doesn't take some long formal prayer. Maybe something as informal as this:

> "Dad, I know we didn't talk a lot about things, but I wanted you to know how much I appreciated all you did for me growing up and as a man. I didn't thank you often. I want you to know today how much I appreciated all the great things you did for me. It made a difference in my life. I am a better man for it. Thanks, Dad."

Put your own words to it and go for it. Your dad is not going to grade you or judge you because it is not about him. You are releasing a burden you have been carrying with you for a long time. Get rid of it. It will give you a deeper sense of peace.

You may have some negatives. Perhaps, these are the ones you need to stop.

Let me ask you the question: "How many more positive traits did you have than negative ones? What if we asked that question to your children or wife? Whoa, careful! It suddenly might get real! I need to add a quick note here. We encourage wives to attend the courses because we find wives are not immune to fathering issues with their dads growing up. We find they become at odds with their husbands about how to father because of their fathering hurts. We ask them the same questions. It is amazing how they better understand how her husband can better father and the supportive role she can play.

I want you to consider this when you finish this book, and you had time to think about all of this. It might be time for you and your wife to be on the same playing field. Consider giving this book to her for her to read. Then, it might be one of those opportunities for you to review this chapter and your answers with her. I will make a promise to you right now. It will do more for your marriage, parenting communication, and your intimacy with each other than any weekend getaway to the mountains. I sincerely hope you will do this. (Another chased rabbit).

In so much of our life, can we trace these traits back to our life teachings, what we have seen, what we have heard, and these things seem to "form" who we are in life? If my dad was an alcoholic, the chances are that I will be an alcoholic. If I have seen my dad hit and scream at my mother, the chances are that I will do the same with my wife. You may have a great dad. I bet you acquired some of his positive traits, as well as his negative ones. Celebrate and be grateful for the positive traits. Those negative ones can be hurting you and the relationship you have with your wife and your children, no matter the age. It is never too late to change some of those things, even if your father is not living.

So, let's move toward a bit more difficult issue.

Why don't you think of a few things that come to your mind that you need to reconcile with your father, whether he is alive or not? Or maybe if you never knew him. For example, for the guy who never knew his father, it might be releasing him for abandoning you as a baby or small child?
You may want to write those down.

Now, it is getting a little stickier. It seems easier to thank someone for a good thing than to face some negative comments that make things more uncomfortable. Remember that we are not talking "crap" about your dad. We are talking about hurts. So, don't go down that road. So, how do you reconcile these things? Sorry, you can't run out on this one. We must reconcile this before we move any further. If there is one vital "key" to moving forward in a positive and fruitful life, we have to empty the trash bag.

This effort does take a bit of bravery on your part. There are several ways to handle this, but in all things, be kind, respectful, and have honor. My best advice is for you to enter the conversation at the right time. Ask God's guidance in giving you the wisdom to provide the right time and place. Do so with respect, humility, and love. If your father has died, write him a letter, go to his graveside or a favorite place you shared in growing up. I am not advocating you talking to a dead person. It becomes more of a symbolic gesture than just saying it mentally to yourself.

Just a few comments. This act of forgiveness is perhaps the most important thing you will do in becoming the father you desire. Remember my story on the way to Africa where I wrote my dad the letter. I did give him the letter on my return with a heartfelt conversation. I asked my wife for advice on what she thought would be a good time. I picked a time to be alone with my dad and was not in public. I made sure I had that talk without my mom around because she would not handle it well. Frankly, I didn't need her to say anything. I knew she might be uncomfortable with this and would try to "make things feel better." My dad had already made considerable changes in his life. Both my brothers knew it, but that was not the point. The issue was I needed to forgive my dad. As with each brother, we all had different but very similar issues with our dad, if not the same life experiences. But this was my problem to resolve.

I needed to let go or release the hurts I had stored up and all that hurt me over the years of my life. Let me be very blunt; if you don't do this important step, this will continue to be your failure. You see, you cannot continue to work through your pain when you talk, work, and play. It is the mask I mentioned. You cannot see through a mask very clearly until you remove it. Then you see life differently with more clarity. The releasing of your hurts is Not for him but for You. So, listen to this: Forgiveness is only about one person – me. For me, I was tired of caring about all the hurts, pain, wounds, or whatever words you choose to use but let's just call it a big suitcase that has weighed me down, and I need to dispose of it. It is hurting me to carry it and deal with all the effects it has on me. It never requires me to go to someone as it is an action between God and me. Now, I am not letting you off the hook because I could do a lot of "mind games" and say in my terms, "been there and done that." The means to physically line up with the offended person has incredible power over your well-being. This action can happen symbolically at a gravesite with a deceased father or eye-to-eye in his living room.

In doing this, you will become free in your life. You will be a better husband and father. When we heal the wounds in our hearts where bitterness, scorn, disappointment, and anger reside and replace them with peace and understanding, you will find joy and relief to move you forward in being a better father. I bet, like me, you will feel a physical relief.

So, with all my heart and encouragement, please find that time and sit with your dad.

Reconciliation

First, let me mention a few things about reconciliation before I tell you how to do it with your dad, son, or wife. For our case, we are discussing how to forgive your dad and have reconciliation with him. Reconciliation is about re-building trust and discussing a plan to move forward in some means or manner. Reconciliation occurs when you are connected spiritually – by God. Sometimes we need a bridge between forgiveness and reconciliation, which is through the means of an apology. It can serve as a means to say that I am willing to move in a positive direction toward reconciling a hurt or wound between us. It can basically mean that we agree to be united and move forward. My experience of mediating a meeting with a father sitting with a son to have this discussion is almost always there is "I am so sorry, and I want to apologize." The groundwork is present to move forward.

Here are some tips to help you.

Realize your father is a son, too. He has been exactly where you have been as a son. We miss this important fact because we have only seen our dad as who he was in our life. I was always intrigued by looking at old photos of my dad as a kid. I always knew him as my dad, not as the young man whose father abandoned him on the highway and told him to hitchhike to the Army Corps for the enlistment of World War II. I have to say I can't even get my head wrapped around what he felt on that highway and the fear he had that he was conditioned to never show or talk about – it is not what Men Do.

Tips for Reconciliation with Your Dad

- Take the initiative
- Don't begin with grievances
- Listen to your father
- Search for common ground
- Tell your dad you care and tell him soon

I can tell you several stories of men across the world who called or emailed me, just devastated that they had been putting off talking to their dad. They were afraid of what they thought might happen (fear). You guessed it. Their dad died before they could visit him. It just broke my heart to listen to a grown man sob, knowing he missed doing the right thing. It can still end up better if you deal with it at the funeral or graveside or leaving that letter in the casket or grave. There is still a huge emotional and physical relief in reading the letter out loud.

Tips for a Meeting with Your Dad

Here is one bit of advice. Remember this is your meeting, and you asked for it. You are to play the central role in controlling the conversation. You are intentional not letting the conversation get into a debate or turn hostile with your dad, not agreeing with your comments, or him being hurt and defensive. Simply remind your dad that you wanted to meet with him, and it was not about him but an opportunity for you to say some things to him. You might not mention you wanted to forgive him until the meeting. Keep the meeting short if he begins to act defensive with words or rebuttal. Simply tell your dad you can talk about this more later. With grace and with love, end the meeting. You will know your dad best. To ease your mind, I have heard of very few instances across the world with men going through reconciliation that a fight or heated argument pursued.

I will give you a small way out on this and say that a handwritten letter given to your dad or mailed to him can be a means to avoid a conflict that you're confident may happen. This is your small out but use it only if your dad might fit into that category, not because you are a chicken! Remember, I used the letter and the conversation. But every meeting going forward was always person to person. Don't involve other brothers and sisters. This is your time.

The letter became my guide and words. I didn't get side-tracked. Over the years, I heard many stories of where the son died due to an accident or war. You guessed it, the dad held onto that letter and even took it to the funeral as though it was the last piece of paper on earth. On the flip side was the man or woman holding their letter from dad. It sort of becomes that moment that "it is all Ok now."

I wanted to spend more time with you on this topic because, in a class, we talk about this one issue probably more than anything else. In fact, we usually spend one half of a day talking about our biggest obstacle in fathering. That is our lack of forgiveness and reconciliation. The most common comment I address with men is how to deal with their dad in either a separated relationship or just a means of improving an existing one. The question is always, "Clark, how do you do it? My dad is a hard man. You don't know my dad. He won't take it well." My only comment is – I bet our dads are a lot alike." You have to break the bolder into small pieces to wash away. Don't continue to talk to the large bolder in fear but attack the fear.

Have you noticed we haven't yet talked about the Seven Secrets? It is because we have to change our hearts to move deeper and stronger into our fathering roles. It is with resolving the past that our future becomes healthy. When we do that, we learn to use tools in a new way. I have learned from too many men who didn't give this topic much seriousness. Here is what happens. The tools became ineffective because the man holding the tool didn't have the right heart to use it correctly.

I want to resay something I just said above this paragraph. You notice I am simply laying down some basic information before we start putting tools in the toolbox. Here is my point: you do not want to buy a new toolbox and put in old, greasy tools, and some are broken and can't work correctly. The tools will not work correctly, and suddenly all the tools and the toolbox are all messed up and dirty. I want you to associate this with Reconciliation with your dad. You cannot move forward with your fatherhood until you clean out your toolbox or replace some of your broken tools – these are what most of us have been carrying around for a long time. Obviously, this is important because I keep hitting you over the head with this reconciliation topic.

So, let's now turn your attention to how you become a Good Father. Let's ask yourself the question, "What does a Good Father look like?" Will you jot down a few things of how that Good Father would look in your mind? Don't cheat reading ahead.

OK, done? Here we go.

What is the Model of a Good Father? The Seven Important Traits of an Effective Father are:

1. COMMITMENT
2. AWARENESS - KNOWING YOUR CHILD
3. CONSISTENCY
4. PROTECTING AND PROVIDING
5. LOVE YOUR WIFE/LOVE YOUR CHILDREN'S MOTHER
6. ACTIVE LISTENING
7. SPIRITUAL AND MORAL EQUIPPING

Today, as at no other time, the influence of the world is playing a major influence on your children. If we don't do what we are designed to do as a Father, our children will find that influence elsewhere.

Friends Replacing Parents

During the 20 years between 1960 and 1980, a dramatic change in family life meant that children became primarily influenced by their friends rather than their parents. We parents buy into that by making sure our children have all the "things" they need to fit in with their peer group. We mistakenly believe that their self-esteem rests on how their peers view them rather than how God views them. There is one secret to preventing drug abuse and overcoming negative peer pressure. That is disciplining your children effectively and raising teens to keep their faith throughout adolescence. That secret is spending large amounts of time with your children. That is essential if we want them to adopt our values instead of those of their peer-group. Gangs or "close peer groups" are the Number One source of replacement kids for identity and a family replacement. If you were to ask Brady why kids join gangs, he would simply tell you that the gang accepts the kid for who he is and not what he did wrong. Gangs do a good job of accepting each other unconditionally. Of course, there are other gang intentions, but it is a good reference point. When we talk with young girls about sex before marriage, it is common that girls will say that the boy said, "he loved her". Of course, with gangs and boyfriends wanting sex, motives usually don't have a positive ending with jail or pregnancy. The overwhelming theme is that kids desire their parents to love them for who they are and refrain from judging the hair color, tattoo, piercings, and clothes. If parents don't find ways to communicate and accept their kids, kids will find another alternative. Statistics show us these kids begin a generational catastrophe for themselves and their kids and their kids.

So, we must learn and apply fathering skills to maximize our relationship with our children.

Applying Fathering Skills

- Make yourself accountable to your wife. Encourage your wife to help you set realistic goals with time and activities. This intimacy becomes critical because both are on the same page with ideas, goals, philosophies, and fathering ideas. When one family deals with conflicts with fights out in the backyard and the other runs from the fight to the closet, you have a big problem being accountable to your wife.
- Make yourself accountable to your kids. Be what you say you are and act accordingly.
- Ask your kids where they see areas of inconsistency with you. Don't be defensive or make snarly faces and listen. They may be giving you the most honest answers you will ever receive.
- Make yourself accountable to other men. Men can affirm and empower each other. Find that man who you can be honest with and talk serious stuff, not a bunch of beer, BS-ing talk, or I am a bigger man than you talk.

I remember giving a talk on a weekend retreat for men. I had given a talk about Brady and me and how Kim and I had been praying for a mentor or shepherd to come into his life until we could better work out differences. I will never forget it when a youth pastor followed me out the door of that conference and stopped me and said, "Mr. Clark. You know you said you and your wife had been praying for a shepherd for Brady to help guide him and be a solid influence on him. I said, sure. He said it's me." And it was. He later convinced his church to hire Brady as an Assistant Youth Pastor. That was the summer Brady influenced hundreds of kids to accept Christ at a summer youth camp. That same Youth Pastor drove Brady to a bible college where he told the college president they were accepting him as a student. Brady's grades were in the toilet, and he didn't qualify. They accepted him. It helped that this same Youth Pastor graduated from that same Bible College as an All-American basketball player and had a lot of influence. My point in this long example is never hinder letting that man enter your life to do what God told him to do. Brady later became an All-American soccer player, graduated, and started a new ministry in Dallas, Texas.

Recognize the Power of the Past

- Resolve issues with your father's fathering of You

Gosh, we have sort of beat this up and so let's move on. The point remains, Resolve issues with your father one way or another.

*The First **Secret of Effective** Fathering is Commitment*

An effective father is one who maintains a long-term commitment as his own. Will you proclaim to the world that your children are yours – your own? Telling your children, they are yours is the first stage of committing yourself to your children.

The first thing you must do is proclaim your commitment to your kids. We do it in many ways, like encouraging your children on the football field and proclaiming to the crowd, "that was my son who scored that point!"

There are Two Parts of Commitment

1. *Dedication Commitment:* This type of commitment is an Internal state of devotion to a person: "I am a Father, and I will stay a father...I am here for my wife and my children." It is a force driving you forward. It communicates a sense of a forward-moving force, a motivation to follow a certain path and give it your best. The loss of dedication commitment represents the loss of a will to try, the loss of a sense of "us," and the loss of the actions that protect a family over time. The loss of dedication removes the passion and life from a father's role.
2. *Constraint Commitment:* This type of commitment brings out a sense of obligation: "I can't abandon my children; I have to take care of them." It is the force driving you from behind. Commitment involves more than claiming your child as your own but resolving to work on your child's behalf. This

requires action: Not just an inner act of the will but also an outer expression of service.

So, why don't you express your commitment today?

Ok, this might be an uncomfortable part, but it is essential that you speak out your commitment. I encourage you to say these things out loud. This may not be the time or place to do so but find a place and do it. I think it would be hilarious and quite cool if you stood up in the middle of a coffee shop or airport and declare:

> *"I am a FATHER, and I will stay a FATHER...I am here for my wife and my children." (Repeat several times)*
>
> *"I can't abandon my children; I have to take care of them." (Repeat several times)*
>
> *If you do this in the middle of a busy airport or coffee shop with enthusiasm and your whole heart and get it on video, I promise you I will use it worldwide at every conference!*

When children hear you state this verbal commitment, it gives them an invaluable point of reference. They feel secure in exploring the world because they always know where home is. They know where they belong. It gives your child a sense of affirmation, communicates belongingness, acceptance, and pride but more than anything, it says, "You are my kid." It is like the example I used earlier of Brady being four years old standing in front of the soccer pitch goal, and I yell, "kick the ball!" And he did but the wrong way. Instead of brow-beating my four-year-old for missing a goal, I should be yelling, "Go, Brady, You're my son!" That would shock the soccer fans, but for sure, everyone would hear me affirming my son.

I believe vocally affirming your kid is one of the most powerful things in the world you can ever do for yourself and your kid. It is a big deal. Kids desire their dad's approval, love, and commitment to them more than anything you can give to them. The point is that kids need to hear you say how much you love them. There is one ugly fact about Brady and me. I did not love Brady unconditionally. I hated his baggy pants, hair color, tattoos, ear piercings, and attitude. Heck, there was just not much I liked about him. This same kid that played soccer and the school play, caught his first fish, jail, rehab, college, sports, and ministry was the same kid in those baggy pants, tattoos, and orange hair. I could never see past my hate for what they represented.

OK, here is a declared rabbit chase:

Years after all this happened, Brady and I frequently spoke at conferences, and one particular event I will remember was in Atlantic, Georgia. It was a huge men's conference, and we were the keynote speakers. We always start our talk together, yelling at each other on the stage as we did in our living room on many occasions. It is so real and ugly that we both almost had flashbacks to the real deal, and let me say, it was real. It was like my dad and big brother I spoke about earlier. After we spoke, a man came up to me and said this: "You know it really bothered me when you said you hated your son. Hate is an ugly word." Before I could think, I said, "Oh, I know, and if there were a word that was worse than 'Hate', I would have used it." Ugly enough, said.

Marital research will show when you combine dedication and constraint in a marriage is like epoxy glue. You get a stronghold bond from the mixing of the two compounds. This is true for fathers if you want to be the most effective father you can be. If you want to enjoy your life as a father, mix your dedication and constraint commitment together. Do you know what is odd about this commitment deal? For the last ten years before my retirement, I had been consulting across Texas. I was not at home as much and certainly disconnected from all the community projects I led in the past. Brady, in the meantime, was hitting home runs with everything he touched. Here is the kid who said he would never return home and was known as a skater kid in rehab. He disappears into rehab, college, ministry and found his way home. Now that I am retired, and we see friends or strangers about town, and they hear my name, guess what they say? Oh, your Brady's dad. I just laugh because everything I had been, Brady has quickly become (the good things), and I quickly proclaim, No, "Brady is My Son." Funny how time fixes most things.

You have heard me throughout the book use the term Effective Father. Why not use the words a Good Dad or a Great Dad? You get the point. Here is your answer. What makes the commitment of an effective father different from that of an ordinary father?

Effective Fathers

1) Effective fathers think about their commitment level, while other fathers may simply try to ward off thoughts of giving up and tossing in the towel.
2) Effective fathers talk to others about their commitment.
3) Effective fathers monitor their commitment level closely. They read the vital signs of their relationship.
4) Effective fathers examine their hearts regularly to see if they are still turned toward their children.
5) Effective fathers differ from other dads. When he finds his commitment ebbing, he actively seeks ways to stimulate it again, like a small group of men having tea or coffee together regularly.
6) Effective fathers have a task orientation toward their fathering. They view their fathering as an occupation.
7) Effective fathers draw confidence from the role of the father itself. We can trust in the relationship of the Father of all fathers established faithful fathering as one of His essential tasks.
8) Effective fathers become more effective when the complexity of the task grows. An effective father rises to meet the challenge. In the face of challenge is simply recognizing that I'm a father, and this is what fathers do. Just because circumstances have become more difficult does not mean that my responsibilities have changed—fathers' father. Committed fathers do their duty. Effective fathers find ways to be effective in the face of adversity and discouragement.

How you approach your fathering commitment is done regularly. Here comes the argument I get from men and especially divorced fathers: I am not with my kid very often, but when we are together, it is great. Hang onto that for a second.

Time

Time is being defined as being involved with your kids, spending time

Time replaces the quality argument. Don't fall into the argument that I am not with my kids very often, but when I am, it makes up for all the times I am gone. The two hours on a Saturday at MacDonald's or a Disney Show make up for not being with them because we have a terrific time. Don't go down that road with me, as you're just trying to make yourself feel less guilty for not finding time to be with them. Watching them grow up and knowing your kid does not happen over a Happy Meal or eating popcorn in a movie every two weeks. There are many ways to connect to a kid in a blended family. There are many books in bookstores everywhere on raising a kid in a blended family. You can refer to our website, where we address this one issue in several of our articles.

An interesting fact to remember: By first grade, kids have spent more time watching TV than talking to his father over a lifetime! Be sure and participate in meaningful activities or what we call everyday stuff and be eager to do so each time. As Kim reminds me, we don't have to go somewhere every time our grandson comes over. We can play a puzzle or word game. I admit it does require taking a deep breath and then doing it. Go to their world and not require them to play in yours.

What was one great thing you did with your dad? Think about it or write it down. I bet you will need some extra paper.

Let's take a moment and go through a Commitment Test. Just answer the questions with a Yes or No.

- Have you consciously and verbally claimed your children?

- *Have you consciously and verbally resolved yourself to act on their behalf?*
- *Are you regularly investing time, energy, and resources in their lives, in a proportion fitting their high place on your list of priorities?*

So, how do you do this? Think about your responses and areas of change required.

ACTION TIPS

- Verbalize your commitment to your kids
- Share your childhood with your kids
- Let your kids know you are accessible
- Assist your kids in activities they enjoy
- Notify others besides your children of your commitment to them
- Take advantage of events in your life as a father where motivation is naturally high to reaffirm your commitment
- Use visual reminders of your children as checkpoints for your commitment
- Surround yourself with some of the "trappings" of fatherhood, such as pictures in your home, in your car, or your briefcase.
- Look for occasions (create them) to have fun with your kids

*The Second **Secret of Effective** Fathering is Knowing Your Child*

You may have the gift of being a good gardener. I would consider myself maybe fair at best. One thing for sure is that to be a good gardener, you must know how to do it.

"If you're planting tomatoes, you're after the fruit."
"If you're planting broccoli, it's the leaf you are interested in."
"If you plant carrots, it's the root."

All of this tells you what fertilizer to use; otherwise, you might have carrots with giant leaves but no roots or tomatoes with deep roots but no fruit. Being a good gardener is like being a good shepherd to your family:

- He calls the sheep of his flock: His wife-kids.
- He knows their strengths, weaknesses, hopes, aspirations – joys, sorrows, and he can minister to their needs.
- His family flourishes.

An effective father knows his children: He studies them and their world, and a part of his motivation is a simple fascination that Kids are Amazing.

But an aware father also wants to gain the knowledge necessary to cultivate his children's unique gifts and talents while protecting his children from what his watchful eye detects.

Knowing How the Garden Grows

Two components:

1. Know how they grow and change. Be very careful not to judge your kids, particularly in sports, if you moved your kids up to a higher division of competition. If he is twelve and the others are fourteen to sixteen years old, he will simply not compete and be as good as the older boys who are well into puberty. So, know where their academic and athletic abilities fit with their age and body and mind development.
2. Developmental awareness. What to expect at certain ages: You need to be aware of the specific knowledge of how all your children grow and change as individuals. In other words, an effective father knows his children in general but also knows his children.

The technical term for General Knowledge is how children grow and change in "developmental awareness":

- Know how they grow and change
- What to expect at certain ages?

Effective Fathers

1) Seek out knowledge
2) Watch their children, nieces, nephews
3) Quiz other fathers
4) Search their non-childhood memory banks
5) Try to stay informed about the different stages of childhood

Your job as a father is to weed out the garden and prepare the right amount of soil so that they flourish and have the full opportunity for growth. To do this, you must know the soil conditions, the plant needs, and what combination brings growth.

Knowing Your Child

- What they are capable of at a certain age
- Knowing individual tastes, goals, abilities, and supporting each one in their unique characteristics.
- Having a good idea of what concerns, problems, and questions a child would have growing up in today's world.

Tending to the Specific Needs of the Garden

The question is: What separates effective fathers from all other fathers is that they are aware of whom their children are as individuals. They know each child specifically. They know what makes their children different from all other children.

What Effective Fathers Know about Their Children?

- When they had a difficult day
- When they were upset about something
- Names of his child's best friends
- What encouraged his child the most?
- When he hurt their feelings
- Knows their strengths and weaknesses
- What motivates:
  - When his child was embarrassed
  - Most of his child's recent disappointing experiences

These are all indicators of a father who knows his children, specifically as individuals. Knowing who your child is helping you as a father to create the conditions for your child to blossom into the uniquely beautiful person God intends them to be. The other main reason why effective fathers pursue knowledge of their children is to help them "ward off things that might hurt their children." Effective fathers get to know their kids for them to come for help in moments of danger and know their susceptibilities.

There are several categories of knowing your child. There is a High to Low end of how we categorize a father in knowing his child."

HIGH END OF KNOWING HIS CHILD

INTRUSIVE: Fathers who describe themselves as involved in every aspect of their children's lives without considering their privacy or individualism can give their children little space to develop their personality.

DISCERNING: Fathers in this group know not only what events are occurring in their children's lives, but they also know how each child perceives these events. These fathers can discern their children's interpretations of the events in the context of their levels of development.

AWARE: This type of father has enough interaction with his children to know the needs, characteristics, and daily happenings of his children. These dads know their children's daily experiences at home, at school, and in the community. They know what to expect from their children relative to each child's age group, and they know how their children compare with their peers. These fathers are aware of specific life events and can see some of these events' meaning for their children.

UNCLEAR: Dads who depict themselves in this manner have some ideas about what is occurring in their children's lives, but these ideas are not specific. They do not know the details of their children's lives and would have difficulty naming their children's friends. These fathers most likely know about the more dramatic events their children experience, but not about the daily occurrences.

UNAWARE: In general, fathers who describe themselves as low in awareness live in a world separate from their children. They often have little knowledge of the issues with which their children are dealing and have little knowledge about their children's school, friends, and personal experiences. These fathers may not be able to describe their children's uniqueness nor know what to expect from them relevant to each child's age group.

LOW END OF KNOWING HIS CHILD

Gardeners Pride and Joy

How important is it for us to be "aware fathers?" You may not realize it until you miss something in your child's life. Being specifically aware of what is going on in your children's lives provides other benefits besides helping us foster their growth and protect them against danger. When you show genuine interest in our children for who they are, you communicate that you consider them important and fascinating. Awareness helps relieve some of the unease we have as fathers. Being aware is simply the joy and fascination that knowing your children can provide.

So, how can we be more aware of the way that they are special and unique?

- Guard your expectations of what they can or can't do.
- Know who your children are as individuals

KNOWING YOUR CHILD IS BEING AWARE

- Do you know what is going on in their world?
- Decide as a family, what are the priorities?
- Do you know your child's favorite color? Song? Show? Friends? Hurts? Joys?

So, let's see how you know your kids by answering a few more questions.

Think about some of your answers. Let's *"Take a moment and think about how well you know your kid or write them in the book.*

What is your child's favorite color? Song? Show? Friend, Hurts? Joys?

Write those down and for a later day, when you see your kids next, ask them the questions and compare your answers to their response. If you're brave enough, ask your wife the same questions and compare her answers with you. I admit straight-up I did poorly. I got the answers to the colors and the names of some of their friends because I hated they wore a lot of black colors. After all, that seemed so negative and ugly. And I am not very proud of the fact that I would have paid for some of their friends to disappear! Fast forward: Some are dead, in prison, and some are great men and women and are very successful. We now laugh with many of them on how I threatened to kill a few of them in my front yard! I drink coffee with many of them, and we now laugh that we all didn't go to jail.

ACTION TIPS

- Simply ask them questions
- Spend time on their turf

- Provide plenty of opportunities for your child to discover their interests and talents and for you to discover them too
- Give feedback about what you observe, especially in Praise
- Get a different angle of your child by listening to your wife, teachers, coaches
- Don't assume your kids are different from others with sex, drugs, and their friends
- Resist focusing on one thing

Conclusion

Please remember to be interested in your kids but don't be intrusive. In developing a perspective of awareness, picture a continuum that extends from being aware of your children to the opposite extreme of being intrusive.

The father, who is unaware, is living in a separate world from that of his kids. There is a free-wheeling father who has abdicated his role. On the other end of the continuum is a formula father who does not respect his child's privacy. When he asks questions, the child senses that the father is not interested in him as a person but checking on him to make sure he isn't stepping out of lines. For a faithful father, questions are a matter of interest; for a formula father, questions are an instrument of control. Where do you sit on the pendulum?

If you remember, in my story, I used many examples of being disciplined or being in the house as my older brother and dad seem to create a battleground of who will win the fight between them. I used the example of retreating to the safety of my bedroom when it seemed the roof was going to blow off our house between my dad and brother's altercations. I would clean my room and closet to ensure everything met my dad's standards, not to trigger an emotion toward me. I don't want you to get lost in the drama of the whipping or my dad's temper. First, it was not like he beat us regularly as some mad man, but when he did, he didn't know when to stop. What is not discussed in this example is my dad having no sense of the damage going on within my heart. He had no clue of the impact fighting had on me as the younger son. He had no sense of the impact of these incidences on my life. The fact of the matter is that he probably never thought about it. He didn't know me. He didn't know how deeply I was hurt. He didn't know or understand how sensitive I was as a little boy who carried forward a sensitive heart as a good trait as a man. This is a great example of knowing your child, but it can be as simple as wanting to take my son to buy some new cleats or football boots for soccer. As the dad, I enter the store and show him new soccer boots, and I never noticed he was looking at a completely different style and color. I had no clue what he wanted and had been shopping in soccer magazines. I was just going to buy him the shoes I thought he should wear on the pitch. I didn't take time to ask or know what He wanted. I never listened to him. It is a simple but huge example of knowing your child.

The Third Secret of Effective Fathering is Consistency

The effective father is defined as one that is consistent. Let's define consistency. Consistency represents <u>predictability</u> in our habits. There is a strong link between trust and security.

A Consistent Dad is defined as:

- One that is representative of regularity and predictability
- There is a strong link between trust and security
- Helps establish marriage as a desirable relationship
- Model working through difficulties in relationships

A Consistent Dad's Demonstration of Consistency

- Governs His Moods: Not affectionate one minute and angry the next
- Keeping of promises
- Morality and ethics
- A daily schedule is predictable

An Inconsistent Dad Is

Emotionally erratic: Kids can't depend on their dad worrying about if he will leave home during a fight.

With effective Fathers:

- Children long for consistency in a fathering schedule and daily habits: Where he is in his day.
- A dad is a reference point that provides security, direction, and confidence in a child's life.

Father, Child, World

When talking about consistency, you have three entities involved, not just two – you are talking about a father, a child, and the world.

Conquering the World with Dad

A Consistent father has unique importance: One of their specific roles as a father is to introduce his children to the world.

The Traditional Model for a child on "going out" into the world has been the father.
The father is one who calls his son and daughter out of the safe confines of the home and into the risks that are in the world. What makes children able to venture out, though, the risks are controlled: The father is out there for them, and he is consistent.

Reference Points

How does a man become a more consistent person and thus a more effective father? Becoming consistent in your moods may prove to be the biggest struggle.

- It is in the struggle dads find victory.

We find that men are inconsistent in their emotions because usually, their fathers were inconsistent.
What do we know about dysfunctional families?

- What they have in common is that they don't know what is normal.
- Children of inconsistent fathers don't know what is normal.
- They don't feel – there is so much pain in a dysfunctional home.

This pain makes kids retreat: They think, "if I don't let myself feel anything, I won't hurt as much." This pain is no different from a father or mother who has lost their kids to the Streets, Gangs, Drugs, Jail, or Death. This picture was very much our story when finally, Kim shut down and checked out with her emotions. In street language, "she was spent." You see, emotions are part of who we are as persons: We can stop our thinking and feeling and cut off our decision-making.

What is done by children of dysfunctional homes?

- Ignore their emotions
- Not allowed to express their emotions

When you relinquish monitoring your feelings and controlling your expression, your emotions have free rein. They swing and shift about erratically and come bursting out at the time of their choosing.

So, emotional expressions are among the most important qualities a father can model. You need to consider that handling your emotions is not the same as hiding them. Dads need to "express" their emotions that the kids see who they are. Our kids always need to see the "feeling" part of you. It is not about your weaknesses; it is knowing when to apologize and sit down and talk to them.

Strong fathers have relationships with other fathers. One of the most important things that will help you is to locate or develop a fathering group. You will find wisdom, encouragement, accountability besides what you saw or not in your father. It takes some coffee, donuts, and then take this text one part at a time, and off you go. The design of this chapter's format is to model a fathering group based on each of the Secrets.

Whatever your faith, seek out the Father and introduce your kid to the spiritual side of their lives. Kids need to understand that The Father is always present, consistent, listen, and you get the idea. Your kid needs to know that the scriptures of your faith become their roadmap. Again, this is why you need to resolve your lingering issues because this has to be real to kids. Kids smoke out BS better than anyone.

There is some difficulty in doing this when they have negative feelings about their earthly father and accepting the heavenly Father. I hope you can begin to see the incredible miracle of Brady extending me grace, forgiveness, and within him also. He is a powerful pastor. Can you imagine the obstacles he and Casey had to overcome with my image of a father and what they had to relearn about the heavenly Father? I stand amazed at that entire process by both of them. Truly God is filled with compassion and love, and the benefit of this truth is what sets us free. In this whole process is that we let God reveal His character to us. We don't have to assume that He is either inconsistent or an authoritarian figure. We can let Him show us that He is compassionate, and we are more inclined to accept Him. A favorite prayer I teach is this: "Heavenly Father, show me what type of Father you are," and God will answer that prayer.

So, relationships with other fathers and the Heavenly Father will give you the encouragement and resources you need to become more consistent in your life.

You will need to take an inventory of these emotions and find the one that causes you trouble. Be vulnerable with your wife and kids, and verbally confess your anger or depression but state that you are working on it. Amazingly, these confessions will help with your consistency. Your kids will see that even if your moods remain for the moment inconsistent, you at least have a consistent desire to work on them.

Keep Your Promises

I post several great clips on our website, and I usually show a few at this point. The movie clips theme is easy: "Never promise anything to a child and not follow through because in that way they learn to lie." When Kim or one of my sons co-teach with me, this is a huge point they make because every day, I would say, "I am coming home, I am on my way," always to get hung up at the hospital. Even though Kim did a masterful job explaining I was staying for a sick patient or some type of emergency, they learned not to really trust those comments from me. Not only did I demonstrate not Keeping My Promise but being Inconsistent.

- One of the biggest problems with promises is forgetting them.
- Intentions are good, but my memory is weak.

The book is full of examples of Dave making promises to my sons and Kim about coming home for supper not to return home until late at night from responding to a sick child at the hospital. For the most part, they could not trust what I said and what I did. In my mind, I felt justified, but in their mind, it was just another day of dad saying something and not following up. Men, make sure what you say is what you do, and I am talking about the smallest of commitments. My kids had the opposite feeling about me. They would know what dad said would never be what dad did as a father or husband. He was all over the map with what he said and what he did. At the end of the day, my family had every right not to trust me or my word. In my mind, I was completely justified, and it was just the fact they didn't understand. I deflected really well.

Guard Your Word

If you begin to find yourself making more explanations than you do fulfillments of promises – you should ask yourself if you are promising too much? I always say go low, and when you are high, you become a winner.

Standardize Your Work Schedule

Your kids will know what to expect from morning to evening and have realistic expectations.

Plan Regular Scheduled Family Time

You have to master controlling the activities around your family – rather than giving something else your prime time and squeeze kids into left-over-time. Your key to this is scheduling. With almost every mobile phone in the world, we tend to carry with us night and day is the ability to set appointments, reminders, and loud alarms to remind us. Use this for your home.

Develop a Hobby, Trade, or Skill

There should be an activity that you all can come back to time and time again and share and talk about it. The shared activity will provide some good time to spend together as a family. It will embrace consistency by giving your children something by which they can define their family. They can define family and know what a family is.

Avoid the Trap of Making Up for Lost Time

Your situation might be about being disappointed in how you've fathered up to this point—may be divorced and living away from kids? Whatever the situation – avoid the urge to make up for the lost time. Don't throw wild extravaganzas because you haven't expressed your love enough lately. When it comes to consistency – you need to realize that those "blow-outs" are a part of a pendulum swing. A month of not hearing from you and then, "bang." If you live away, be consistent with phone calls, letters but being predictable and regular. Kids need a firm feel for where home is, and they feel they know what they'll find when they get there.

ACTION TIPS

- Keep your promises
- Guard your word
- Standardize your work schedule
- Plan regularly scheduled family time
- Develop a hobby, trade, or skill that everyone can enjoy
- Avoid the trap of making up for the lost time

You remember I commented on some of the Secrets you will score high and some low. I can say about this secret if there was a rating below zero, that was me. I miserably failed in this, and why? I got work drilled into me. If you look back at my summary before starting the course, 99% centered around work.

Now, why don't you think about or write down three areas you need to be more consistent in with your children and your wife.

Let's keep going. Don't quit on me.

Day Two

*The Fourth **Secret of Effective** Fathers is Protecting and Providing for Their Families.*

Today, there seem to be so many threats in today's world that cause corruption and danger for kids that will steal their lives and hearts. The stakes are high when our children's eternal destinies hang in the balance. Some of the ways we guard against that is protecting our young girls and boys with their sexual innocence. Our young girls and boys are bombarded with sexual stimulation and information. Our homes must be protected by our presence. More than 2/3rds of teens quit practicing their faith by the time they leave their teen years because of one fatal torpedo, and that is sexual immorality. This is one issue that both teens and adults think they can engage in without damaging their faith. Three out of five teens that have sex do so at home when their parents are away, and four out of five students who drink do so at their friends' houses or parents' houses when they are away. But before fathers can protect their teens, they must protect themselves. Fathers need to include themselves in their protective instincts. Divorce not only rips apart a marriage, it usually tears a father from his children. Absent fathers cannot protect their children. The most common marriage buster is adultery. If you love your children and want to protect them, then remain faithful to your wife by guarding your eyes and watching your actions---very carefully. But the basic principle in providing and protecting is that you can't do the job you are destined to do when you aren't there.

Responding in Time of Crisis

Some protective issues may be less visible than in the days of the past when we fought with spears, arrows, and guns compared to protecting:

- Our employment
- Wife's sickness
- Child's drug habit
- Property

Protection seems to have taken on a bigger dimension of thinking than just protecting our family and our house like on a Western television show.

We might want to look at what a minor crisis may include:

- Scraped knees
- Lost pet
- Broken household item
- Lost toy

Being able to respond to a crisis is not as easy as it takes fortitude and commitment.

The ways to ensure protection:

- Children know First Aid principles during times of a swimming accident or bleeding
- They need to know how to protect themselves in knowing how to swim or stopping bleeding.
- Know how to contact a family member
- How to dial emergency numbers for help
- Computer safety

You get the idea, and you can add it to this list. List a few and add them to this list.

What I Saw My Father Do?

A father's positive response is crucial in an indirect way. As kids experience their crisis – they all remember how their dad responded or modeled how to handle a crisis. A father must model the type of grace under pressure that he wants his children to emulate. Our protector, as a father, will extend beyond our presence. Can you remember the story of my dad coming up to the school when the Dean of Men was going to punish me with butt swats, and my dad intervened?

Six Things Effective Fathers Do That Help Make Them Better Protectors of Their Children

1) Adopt a Healthy Attitude Toward Crisis
   - First, effective fathers recognize that crisis will occur and are not caught off guard
   - Second, effective fathers accept beforehand that one of their roles as a father is to be a protector. They are ready to step forward and act when necessary.

- Third, effective fathers believe that the strength gained from the family crisis can be greater than the harm suffered.

2) Identify the Role Models from When You Learned How to Deal with Crisis
   You can watch and listen to others going through a life crisis and learn to empathize with their situations. This will allow you to think about how we would respond and plan the best way to reach out to those in need. If we can objectively think through a disaster that affects others, we can begin to develop plans for responding positively when a crisis strikes closer to home.

3) Regain Your Confidence After a Crisis by Enjoying the Support of Other Fathers
   Being a father is tough. Fathers can gain confidence in their plans and decisions through the support of other fathers.
   - No one is born with fully developed fathering skills – so there will be failures.
   - The support of other fathers can enable you to gain back your confidence.
   - Confidence helps you create an atmosphere of stability.

4) Understand Your Foundations as a Man
   The National Center's studies show that fathers able to deal with crises also responded well to male identity issues. In other words, they related the handling of the crisis to feel comfortable being a man. A good motto on the door of the kitchen icebox could be: "Be A Man and Fight Against the Crisis in Your Home." Take confidence in how God has created you. When a crisis occurs, simply say, "This is it! It is for occasions just like this. I am a father and a man."
   Are you satisfied with your roles as a male? Are you comfortable being head of the household, or do some of the responsibilities make you feel insecure? Insecurity leaves men vulnerable to crisis. Fathers who are firmly grounded in their masculinity and who feel good about themselves are willing

to go through a crisis and more likely prepared when one does occur.

5) In Times of Crisis, Talk with Your Children
Fathers who deal successfully with crises have healthy verbal interaction with their kids. You can talk through, during, and after a crisis.

The effective father can openly communicate with his children. His children feel they have an open channel to their dad at any time concerning a subject. Maybe a solution has been discovered by the attentive ears of fathers who can obtain and utilize their children's collective insight. Daily interaction with our kids has rewards that extend far beyond the potential benefits it brings in solving the crisis.

6) Maintain a Consistent Discussion with Your Wife, as well as Your Kids
Effective fathers who have a healthy interaction with their wives are familiar with their mates' special ability and know-how to utilize those assets in a tense situation. The importance of healthy marital interaction is shown graphically during the crisis. Couples who have lost a child are more likely to divorce than couples who have not faced such a disaster. When a crisis occurs to `parents who communicate regularly with one another – they can get positive results. Husbands who ideally have strong communication habits already established with their wives; their discussion will be a natural response in a crisis.

ACTION TIPS

- Adopt a healthy attitude toward the crisis
- Identify the role models from whom you learned how to deal with the crisis
- Regain your confidence after a crisis by enjoying the support of other fathers
- In times of crisis, talk to your children

- Maintain consistent discussion with your wife, as well as your kids

Providing

As fathers, you must assume the primary responsibility for the financial provision of your families. You must seek to learn and apply sound principles of financial stewardship within your families. Whenever possible, you must strive to provide the maximum opportunity for your wife to nurture. As fathers, we will protect our families from physical, spiritual, and moral harm. We will protect them from everything that disturbs or destroys the fragile nature of innocence and purity.

A Roof Over Their Heads

- Providing financially for your family is related to protecting them.
- When you provide a roof over their heads, you protect them against the weather.
- When you provide money for food, you protect them from starvation
- When you pay taxes, you protect your children against crime since a portion goes to protection.
- What effective fathers tell us is that you should not feel guilty about going to work – unless you never come home from work, but while doing your jobs and drawing your paycheck, you should feel proud that you are faithfully fulfilling your roles as fathers.
- The question is, "what if you lost your job – how would such a loss affect your relationship with your kids? Would you feel like a poor father?
- The question is not, should you feel like you were a poor father, but would you? It seems to be an issue of fathering motivation and satisfaction. Studies show that that as

the economic sufficiency of these men grew, there was a corresponding increase in the active participation they had with their children.
- The way fathers respond to economic loss affects their relationship with their children.
- Fathers who responded more irritably and with pessimism to a loss were more punitive and less nurturing in their children's interactions.

Financial Provision is Important

The best advice an effective father can give you is "to get a job and keep a job."

What Effective Fathers are Not saying?

They are not saying that making more money leads to greater fathering satisfaction. In fact, by statistic, the effective fathers were in the middle-income bracket. The income level is not as important as having a steady income that provides for the family's basic needs. Effective fathers are saying they don't have to be the sole provider for the family. Effective fathers bring to their provider role the knowledge of their family's needs. They begin with an understanding of what it will take to support their wife and kids and what it will take to foster their children's aspirations; this understanding then governs the choice of their place in the workforce. When you begin with knowledge of your family's needs and then make a career choice, you gain some wonderful advantages. First, you will help relieve the tension caused by a perception that your workweek is competing against your home life. Second, when you know your needs and then make choices based upon them, it's easy to determine whether you are successfully providing for your children.

Providing in A Challenging Economy

Our world economy is becoming more and more complex. The dream of most men is to simply do better than their fathers. Effective fathers are rewriting the dream to say, "We can exceed our fathers." They have translated the dream from performance first to relationship. Committed dads are saying to their children, "We're here to help one another." They are pulling together in a spirited camaraderie of survival similar to what we experience in many homes during years of depression or famine. They are pooling resources together for each other's good. What distinguishes effective fathers from all other dads is that they know their children's needs and then work to meet those needs. Effective fathers know early on what their children's plans and dreams are. They provide steady encouragement to those plans and dreams as the child grows and then work to provide the necessary education to support those dreams.

*The Fifth **Secret of Effective** Fathering is Loving Your Child's Mother*

> "Through union with a woman, children are born."

> "Through communication with that same woman, secure and confident children are born."

This secret poses many issues in today's world of high divorce and out-of-wedlock births with damaged families in our world. Of the world's 140 million births that happened in 2016, about 15 percent or 21 million – were born out of wedlock. The effect on our children is devastating.

There is little room for variance in this secret.

What about fathers whose wives have left them?
There are some interesting facts in the United States, with half of our marriages end in divorce. Studies are now demonstrating that

women initiate 80% of divorces. Worldwide statistics aren't readily available or reliable, and cultures will play a significant role in their view of divorce.

How can these men apply this secret after they have experienced marital disruption?

This secret creates great difficulty for those men who sincerely love their children and want to be effective dads but have a hard time loving their children's mother. Certainly, many people argue that the father-child relationship is one relationship and the husband-wife relationship is another, and that one can remain strong despite the other. Interestingly, the most significant political issue regarding fathering uses this premise. There are court cases with gay couples being allowed to adopt, equal rights for dads, custody battles. The premise is that the father-child relationship exists independently of the husband-wife relationship.

Despite the arguments that children in single-parent homes can succeed in the same way's children in two-parent families, the best researchers will readily point out that children of single-parent families have more obstacles to overcome. Statistics reveal that single mothers live in levels like poverty levels and kids are more likely to be:

- More sexually active
- Give in to more peer pressure
- Abuse drugs and alcohol
- Score lower on school exams

In reviewing this curriculum, we could say that Dads are important, and I will say right behind that, so are mothers. At the very least, we must admit that if it were not for a woman, no man could become a father. But we don't go far enough unless we also acknowledge that a strong marital relationship will help a dad become a highly effective father. A strong marriage does much to help you fulfill your fathering role. We can break this fifth secret of effective fathers into two components: Marital Interaction and Parental Discussion.

Marital interaction is simply the loving bond that you have with your wife. When you strengthen it, you provide an atmosphere of security in your home, where your children grow. You also model what an effective marriage looks like and determine how your children perceive marriage and whether they will eventually be successful when they get married.

Parental discussion is the second fathering component that includes your wife. When you discuss your children with your wife and get feedback from her on your fathering, you create a parenting team that uses your collective wisdom in raising the children.

One of The Best Things You Can Do for Your Kids

Marital interaction means focusing on your children by focusing on your wife. This action may seem indirect, but your children will be the ones who receive direct benefits. Studies show that marital quality is a predictor of a father's ability to give positive feedback. If the father had low marital satisfaction, he was more likely to be intrusive in father-child interactions and give less positive feedback to his children. While we may be inclined to separate husband-wife and father-child interactions into two different relationships, studies show that it is not easy.

The quality of marital life gives a long way toward determining our communication with our children, the sexual protection of our children, our commitment to and satisfaction with our children, and our children's ability to handle crises.

Do You Love Your Kids?

Well, one of the best things you can do for them is to love their mother. The main benefit to your children of good marital interaction between you and your wife is an atmosphere of security.

Father and mother are the leaders of the household. They originated the family, and all the children take their cues from them. Though marriage is not the only relationship in the family, it is certainly the first and the most important. If the atmosphere of the marriage is distrust, the atmosphere of the family is distrust. If the atmosphere of the marriage is anger, the atmosphere of child-rearing is anger. If the marriage atmosphere is noncommunication, the atmosphere in which the children grow is silent and foreboding.

The Opposites Hold True

Like all secrets of effective fathers, strong marital interaction continues to bear fruit in a child's life long after the child has left home. Parents who have a strong marriage are also modeling strong marital interaction. Your modeling of a loving marriage influences many of your children's perspectives and practices in their marriages.

Teamwork

The other aspect of fathering that involves your wife is parental discussion. If marital interaction is where you and your wife come together as one to focus on each other, the parental discussion is where you come together – also as one – to focus on your children.

Here are the questions that effective fathers should answer in the affirmative:

1) Do you discuss your children's development with their mothers?
2) Do you discuss your children's problems with their mother?
3) Do you discuss goals for each child with your child's mother?
4) Do you discuss your frustrations as a parent with your child's mother?

Now, if you were able to answer these questions with a Yes, then you've discovered that of all your fathering assets – which your child's mother is at the top of the list. You have discovered that you are not alone. Plus, you and your child's mother can form a parenting team that can work effectively for your child's benefit.

We ask fathers in our surveys, "What person contributed most in helping you overcome difficulties in your fathering?"

- Some listed their fathers, other male friends, or even their pastor.
- Some listed prominent celebrities
- The overwhelming answer was "my wife."

The synergy itself is remarkable. Women have done an admirable job of raising the past generations of children. In many cases, by themselves, as many men relinquished their father's role and were blind to the long-term satisfaction of being actively involved in the family. BUT no matter how good a mother she might be, she can't also be a father. Only a father can be a father. The wives can assist in a father being a better father. There are three things that your child's mother can provide you with through parental discussion:

1) She can provide you with additional data about your children. She will do things and go places while you are at work. When you have that time at the end of the day or early in the morning, "You will ask, so, how is Susie?"
2) She can provide you with a different perspective on your children. You may only see parts of your child due to time, but your wife can tell you other things from being with the child longer and see things you might never see. She will have a different perspective.
3) Regular discussion with your wife can yield tips on how to improve your parenting skills. One study reported that a father's lack of fathering skills is often linked to increased marital conflict.

The reason that these fathers lack parenting skills is that they shut themselves off from the most knowledgeable teachers of parenting - their wives. Ask for advice and listen; ask for feedback. It is easy to be blind to our strengths and weaknesses. Sometimes the most profitable question you can ask is, "How am I doing?" A father who discusses his fathering skills with his wife gains a great deal of confidence.

Over-protective Mom Issues

Usually, there are issues relating to a woman abandoned by a father or father wounds that transport into present relationships. One of our key objectives in fathering courses is to include women or wives, Sunday School Teachers, etc. because fathering wounds passed down from father to daughter are real and frequent. We must do a better job of educating couples on their job descriptions, so battle lines don't happen in the heat of a child-problem because of past hurts and habits.

Remembering Our Roles

Mom and dad are leaders of the household
Family is more than just an organization but an organization where husband and wife have become one and where the children are our flesh and blood.

> If there is an atmosphere of distrust = the atmosphere of the family is distrust

> If there is an atmosphere of love = the whole family will absorb that love.

Enhancing the Marital Bond

Having a plan to enhance your marital bond is as important as having a plan to interact with your children. Take time for just the two of you, and sometimes it is just REST you need than a fast trip somewhere.

I wanted to add at the end of this secret comments verbalized in every class regarding this secret. It involves a man that is divorced. I am sure if you are divorced, you may be thinking about this also. Here comes the typical question: "Dave, let me see if I understand you, right? You want me to love that woman who ran around on me with different men, lied to me, and broke our marriage covenant by adultery? You totally don't get it. I would rather see her burn in hell." I stand amazed at how a husband or wife married for years who know everything about each other down to the birthmark location on their bodies, and they talk and act like total hateful strangers. In a divorce, we seem to bring out rocket launchers firing deadly missiles loaded with venom and hate. As I smile and say back to him, "Absolutely, I am not asking you to have sex, agree with her on everything, but you have to demonstrate to your child that you love their mom." And the same is true with the mom loving the father. She is still the mother, and you are the father. Both need to work on your kids' goals and consider including the new spouses in the new marriages. All of the partners need to be together in setting realistic goals for all the kids. I will not disagree that a blended family will have huge obstacles, but it can be successful. You have to agree on what is best for the child. Just remember that the one agenda is the kid, not out of control, and manipulative adults.

ACTION TIPS

- Repeat your wedding vows often so your wife and children can hear them regularly
- Show affection for your wife in front of the kids
- Date your mate
- Take your kids with you when you go shopping for a gift for your wife
- Don't make your wife suffer unnecessarily for the sake of the children

The Sixth Secret of Effective Fathering is Active Listening

For many dads, listening is one of the most frustrating stumbling blocks. Listening – really listening is more than just a moment's attention but something that takes time. We need to hear all that our children need to say. Effective fathers have learned the discipline of actively listening to their children.

Finding Meaning in the Mayhem

Unfortunately, in your home and your life, your kids are competing against all sorts of noises, distractions, electronic devices, and crises within the family. You have control over all of this if you would just do it. The goal is to learn to tune out and focus your attention at those times when you especially need to listen to your children.

Selective Hearing

There are so many noises surrounding a father – pressures and demands, schedules, and to-do lists. At times these noises seem to crescendo and drown everything else, but the fact is that at any given moment, you choose what you want to give your attention.

So, let's try something right now. Put everything down and listen to the sounds around you. What did you hear?

Traffic, wind, and the list go on. All these noises were occurring even before you stopped to listen to them. If you did not notice them before, it was because you chose to focus your attention, perhaps on my words.

Let's Look at the Skills of Attentive Listening

- Face your child squarely
- Adopt an open posture
- Put yourself on your child's level by squatting down and, if possible, leaning toward
- Maintain good eye contact
- Stay relaxed as you listen
- Learn to read our child's nonverbal behavior
- Give non-verbal feedback by nodding/making your eyes light
- Respond to your child by restating in your own words what has been said

Dad, often your best approach to a child's problems is to listen. Maybe after listening, you can determine that what your child needs most is a big daddy hug – not advice. Fathers need to listen. Children need to be heard. And children respond to their attention.

If you want to win with your kids – listen. What makes listening so important is that it feeds all our other fathering roles. It is a foundational discipline for fathering activities.

Showing Affection

- Many fathers show affection in their children: Hugging and saying, "I love you."
- But for effective fathers listening is a sign of affection.
- Active listening to your kids communicates to them that you consider them unique enough to deserve your undivided attention. You are expressing to them that they are worthy of being known and understood.

Knowing Your Child

- We have already discussed how one of the 7 Secrets of effective fathers is awareness of how our children are developing.
- An effective father knows who his kids are, what are their strengths and weaknesses, their gifts and talents, and what motivates and discouraged them.
- How do you gather information? By listening. You simply look them in the eyes and, in your fashion, say, "Tell me about yourself," and then sit back and take it all in.
- If a father is involved in his children's lives and is a regular listener, there will be times when the information is upfront and straightforward.
- But we need to understand that these open, honest moments will never occur unless the father proves himself as a listener during the other moments. The only thing that seems to be happening is somewhat tedious chitchat.
- A child who finds his father open to the small things will be more willing to share the big things with him.

Motivation

Statistically, strong listening behaviors are usually linked to motivation. Research has examined men who claimed they were highly satisfied with their fathering. The one quality or skill that was connected most directly to fathering satisfaction was verbal interaction. The father who talks with and listens to his children gets the most satisfaction as a dad. What is it about listening to that feeds your motivation as a father? It allows you to experience the purest joy of being in a relationship: Intimacy. You get to connect with another being who is important to you. Another reason may be the honor you feel at being taken in as a confidant. Active listening also embraces your motivation because it protects you from that awful sense that your children are concealing deep, dark secrets that they might spring on you at any moment.

Fathers who don't listen have good reason to foster such fear. Active listening does its greatest work for your motivation as fathers by helping relieve you of one of your greatest fears: that you, as a father, need to have all the answers. Knowing we don't have all the answers is not the issue. The key is understanding that kids are looking for a chance to express themselves to get a vote of confidence or a listening ear, or a sign of love. Many find their answers once they use the opportunity as a sounding board.

Turn Down the Noise

The term active listening is not a passive pursuit. You are actively seeking to understand what your children are thinking and feeling. That may mean turning off the noise and then get into the listening position where you ask questions for inquiry or clarification or to repeat something to make sure there is a connection. The term focused attention means that you are giving your child undivided attention in such a way that he feels without a doubt that he is completely loved. This type of attention is directly related to a child's self-esteem. Listening is a discipline that you can learn and at which you can become more proficient. Effective fathers are craftsmen at listening.

Turn Down the Noise by Removing Physical Distractions

When you are attempting to listen to someone, you need to be able to do two things:

1. Hear the words they're saying and concentrate on those words. When your kids approach you with something to say – get things off for their attention.
2. Removing physical distractions not only helps us as listeners but also encourages our children as speakers.

What is the biggest obstacle? TV. Just turn the damn thing off and leave it off. It cannot be a substitute for family time, communicating, and learning more about each other and their life for the day. The same goes for the cell phone. Turn it off!

Turn Down the Noise by Blocking Out the Demanding Voice of Your Schedule

- Active listening requires time.
- Focused attention means being willing to hear all that your children want to say.
- Active listening includes the gift of your time, communicates love and respect.
- Generous time also aids you as a listener.
- Be smart when and how the conversation needs to be delayed without being unconcerned.
- The dynamics of active listening are another argument for the superiority of quantity time over quality time: the more time you give your child, the more opportunity to listen.

The purpose of active listening is to gain understanding.

- Simply listen and seek to understand.

Sympathy and Empathy

Sympathy says, "Oh, I feel the same way you do," while Empathy says, "I understand how you feel." We are not called to sympathy as listeners; we are called to empathy. You don't have to agree with your child's misguided thinking, but you should seek to respect him or her by seeking to understand what he or she is experiencing.

Let patience rule. Interestingly, a famous person once wrote this powerful reminder: "Everyone should be quick to listen, slow to speak, and slow to anger." The purpose of active listening is to achieve an understanding of what your children are thinking and feeling. To do that: Ask thoughtful, open-ended questions that gain more information, and that clarifies your understanding. Stay away from cross-examination and begin building your case. The goal is empathy: Ask, "how did it make you feel?"

Turn Down the Noise by Not Preparing and Practicing Your Intended Speech While Your Child is Talking

Your goal as an active listener is to get a handle on the situation and formulate an opinion of what should not be done. Your final goal is to gain an understanding of how your child perceives the situation. Ask clarifying questions without making statements that prematurely "cut off" the talk from the child. Listen for the agenda: Listen to what the child is trying to say. Look beyond the words and try to listen to what is going on in the heart. Just remember that communication is the "lifeblood" of relationships. When a father fails to listen to his children, it can shut down his relationship with them indefinitely.

ACTION TIPS

- Remember Active Listening is not a passive pursuit/TURN DOWN THE NOISE
- Turn down the noise by blocking out the demanding voice of your schedule

- Turn down the noise by not preparing and practicing your intended speech while your child is talking
- Whenever your child speaks, always keep this question in mind: "What is the Agenda? Listen to the Heart."

The Seventh **Secret *of Effective*** *Fathering is Spiritual Equipping*

As there are many faiths across the world with different beliefs, I will address primarily a target population that will include those that believe in a God, Supreme Being, Father, or whatever words you place on that figure in your faith. This book applies to a Muslim dad or any man of other faiths where we want every dad to have his father toolbox. Obviously, from reading this book, I am probably what you would consider an evangelical Christian. Let me be very clear that it is probably what people might label me as with places I worship across the world and my faith principles. But let me be very clear, I am by label a Christian, not what some faith body labels me. Simply put, I am a part of the larger Body of Christ throughout the world, whatever they like to call themselves or what name they put on a sign outside a building. None of that has much value when it comes to the Father and me.

Here is my point of clarity. The focus of the last secret is understanding the spiritual aspects of a child's relationship with God. I would think by now in the book, my speaking of my life and faith experiences could be an obstacle for you if these are contrary to your faith belief structure. I think you might have tossed the book by now. So, let's move on to the last tool in your toolbox.

The last secret's focus is for fathers need to understand the spiritual aspects of their children's relationship with God.

Spiritual Inadequacy

Understandably, many fathers feel inadequate when it comes to spiritual matters. We're surrounded by many other people who seem much better equipped than we are to foster our children's growth.

What we find about men is that seems easier to delegate spiritual responsibilities to our wives, but we need to embrace our fatherly role as spiritual fathers. Even though our kids may be surrounded by Godly people from the church or family, the father must be a part of the team. You cannot abdicate your role as helping your child connect to his spiritual life. At the end of the day, the responsibility of raising kids in our faith principles rests with you. Research shows us that men tend to look at spiritual leadership as an outward display. It cannot be about just going to a building of faith but having a deep relationship with the Heavenly Father. So much of spiritual equipping is modeling. Another famous author wrote that faith without deeds is useless. The best judge of growth is your kids and wife. Dads must instill beliefs in their kids. One of the most common disagreements fathers have with their kids is they don't seem to agree on religious principles primarily because it never gets talked about with the dad. Remember my story when I said that even though we were very involved in church activities, there was an absence of devotions and prayers as a family.

There are Four issues to deal with in Spiritual Equipping

1) How important is it for my children to be spiritually equipped?
2) How important is it that I, the father, be a spiritual leader?
3) In what ways has God already equipped me as a father to be suitable for the task?
4) In what ways can I prepare myself further to be an effective spiritual equipper?

The question about spiritual equipping is not whether your children will have a relationship with God, but what type of relationship they will have with Him. Your children can be a stranger to Him or a close companion. The question is how well or how poorly this aspect of their lives will develop. For too long, parents have ignored the spiritual equipping of their children. Today we reap the consequences. The great motivation for spiritually equipping our children is to teach our children how to gain the whole world without sacrificing their values and integrity.

No Place Like Home

There is a significant historical pattern that established the father as a spiritual leader in the home. For the people in ancient history, faith assemblies or churches aren't as much as we see them today. But in all our faiths, we know that nations were made up of tribes, and tribes were made up of families. In all our faiths, we are taught to love our God with our whole heart and soul. Our faiths instruct us how to teach the children to "repeat these words to your children. We are taught to discuss the scriptures and their meaning as families in homes or where we travel.

God intended his instruction to be part of the day-in-and-day-out routine of family life. The responsibility for introducing the children to the mysteries of the faith fell primarily upon the homes and only secondarily on the faith community. The manner of instruction seems largely informal: Fathers taught as the opportunity presented itself in the daily walk of life. Most of the children of our faith are referred back to their parents to listen and follow their instructions. Men are taught not to exasperate their children but bring them up in the Father's kindness and guidance.

The responsibility for spiritually equipping children resides primarily with parents and with the public assembly only secondarily. Another author states that the father would talk with his child, be encouraging, listen with your heart, and challenge them to live responsible lives worthy of God who calls us all into his kingdom. A father needs to encourage or to speak words of blessing and to comfort (listening to and understanding concerns) but also urging or helping his children understand the significant role they play in the kingdom of God. This urgency in spiritual matters is vitally important for fathers to express.

The Missing Part of the Spiritual Team

The wife has played a major role in the home and the church; the father needs to join his wife just as he does the church. We eluded earlier that the father is the one who introduced the children to the world. At the same time, the mother is identified with the home.

It seems the mother is the one who teaches the children about the gracious compassion of the Father. Of course, for boys who grow up without a masculine model of spiritual vitality in the home, there is the inclination to conceive a faith belief as a feminine pursuit. The workplace has done well in calling men through specific tasks and rewards for a job well done. The faith community has had a tough time calling men out to live lives of faith. A father's presence among your children will affect their spiritual views. Your examples of servanthood and discipleship go long ways for your children to understand your role and to understand you don't have all the answers. Feeling inadequate becomes strength when you are honest about it.

Equipping Yourself to Equip Your Children

Working from a position of strength, you can now ask yourself: In what ways can I equip myself further to be an effective spiritual equipper of my children? The first answer is to grow in your faith and mature in your relationship with God. So how do I do that? Don't underestimate the power of living a holy life by modeling the truth: Guard your integrity and practice what you preach. Get feedback from your wife and kids: Guard against being defensive. Lead your family in worship by being together and pray together. When you participate in worship, you focus on someone outside of yourself who can bring a calming effect to all the responsibilities you intuitively feel. This practice exceeds all understanding. Lead your family in worship by honoring the church service by ensuring your family is ready for worship not only physically but mentally, emotionally, and spiritually to hear God speak. Have time afterward as a family and talk about it or just rest in the experience of it. Lead your family in worship at home and have time for devotion, prayer time, communion, reading of the scriptures while being careful not to equate spiritual equipping with "being in control" and not about keeping everyone in tight control. All families mess up: Good or bad

Raising our children to be effective in their faith is too important a task to delegate to someone else.

Effective fathers rise for the challenge, confident that God will make up for their weaknesses and bless even the most uncertain efforts. Parents are the first and primary educators of their children. Fathers are particularly singled out in our faiths for the spiritual education and training of their children regardless of their faith. It is simply the order of things. The high privilege and duty of fathers teaching the faith to their children will result in a faith that will persevere through adolescent questioning, peer pressure, and school life.

So, let's answer a few more questions: Think about your answer or write them down.

- *Do you pray with your wife daily?*
- *Do you pray for your kids or grandkids by name daily?*

Spiritual Equipping

This is the primary responsibility of parents and the Father. Usually, the missing part is the Father. Just remember that you don't have to be perfect. Be honest about your struggles and your trials and make their spiritual journey real also.

How Does That All Happen?

- Realize that God commissioned you.
- He knows we are all inadequate. He describes Himself as a father.
- He gave us other men and fathers encouragement and accountability (small groups).
- Pray with your wife.
- Pray for your kids and grandkids by Name.

ACTION TIPS

- Pray out loud.
- Be equipped in the Word.

- Lead your family in prayer and devotions.
- Your life serves as the model.

Whew...

You received a very candid version of "The Seven Secrets of Effective Fathers." Your toolbox should have seven great tools to equip you with almost everything in being an effective father. You will learn different things as you grow in fatherhood. I would encourage you to place those newfound tools in your toolbox and open it frequently. You remember I told you my little brother has the prized toolbox after our dad's death. All three brothers used various tools in my dad's toolbox for most of our lives. We remembered to put most back for the son or daughter behind us. It was not about having all the original tools we remember being in the toolbox as we grew up. We remember most of them and how my dad had used them in our lives. He freely gave away many of his tools because a man might have needed them at that time of his life. And we used them with our kids one by one. Your toolbox will grow and shrink as time goes on, but the key is to hand off that toolbox to the one you feel needs it the most. After all, it might have been for a guy like me who was broken, discouraged, and empty. He might have been that man who just needed a tool to replace the ones he realized were broken, or he simply didn't have any tools. That man needed someone just to walk up and say, "You know, I got a tool in my toolbox that has worked for me, you want to borrow it? But there is just one little rule – "you give that tool away to the next Dave." You will find, with each tool or secret, that you have mastered it well, and you need to share it to keep it sharp and in good working condition. There may be one or two that you will need to study the instructions with the tool to know how to use it well – you now have the instructions. As time goes by, you will go from tool to tool, using some more, and some will just be used naturally without instruction or maybe your wife reminding you how to use it. A bit of a secret from me to you: I keep several toolboxes ready to give away for the one who thinks he needs it the least but needs it the most.

Now you know about commitment, knowing your child, consistency, protection/providing, loving your child's mother, active listening, and spiritual equipping. Your next stage enters the phase in which you begin to apply what you have learned. You have learned what your strengths and weaknesses are. It might be time in the story for you with me to consider committing or recommit to fathering. Just believe that these seven secrets will stand you on solid ground, but there is one thing you still lack.

I need to tell you about the eighth secret (one more tool), believe it or not, the eight of the seven secrets of effective fathers. Stay with me.

As we talked about gardening, we discussed how a plant grows, fertilizing it, and watering it. And it grows. What brought about this success? Many people will say it was the weather, the right soil, the right seed, and proper cultivation. And you ask the question, "What is life?" What causes it to grow?

Some say, "It just happens." "God does it." And one says, "It is a mystery." You never know when there is a drought to come along and ruin it or more rain – ultimately, it is out of our control. As fathers, we must admit that there is no guarantee that our children will turn out the way we want them to. They are human beings who make their own choice – and there will be surprises. Fathering is a complex task, and perhaps more than we bargained for when we held our wife in a loving embrace that night, we conceived a child.

Like the farmer, he can do the best of everything he knows to do. He knows if he is faithful, he can feel confident that he'll reap a plentiful harvest, but he will admit there are no guarantees.

But what if you decide to do nothing at all? And the answer is I'd get nothing – no crop at all.

So, it is with fathering. On the one hand, you can do your part by applying the seven secrets of effective fathers. You will likely reap a crop of well-equipped children who live their lives wonderfully before God, though there is no guarantee that this will happen. On the other hand, you can choose to wither in the face of uncertainty and apply none of the fathering principles that you learned or those from other men or yourself.

If you opt against faithfully doing what you know you need to do, then you have created your guarantee in fathering – the guarantee of failure. We all need to apply the seven secrets of effective fathers and humbly allow the rest to remain a mystery.

What is the Eighth Secret?

I have No idea, but it's a mystery. We cannot reduce fathering to a series of foolproof steps leading to instant success. So, we just must confess there are things we just don't know.

Each of us may possess this Eighth Secret. Maybe we just can't verbalize it to each other or even to ourselves. When it comes to fathers, there is a secret within each father that longs to express with his kids, and it normally allows for some shared memories to develop between a father and child. This secret may be the most profound of them all. It is each man's expression of his fathering. It may come at a time, you least imagine. Let me take you back to an earlier chapter. It was about some of my stories about premature babies, life-flight helicopter flights in the middle of the night, and all the blood and guts that were such a part of my life. I tell stories to friends that I have heard more things from people in their final moments of death that will shake your very foundation of life. In so many cases, I could take you back to that room or hospital or wreck site on the side of the road to hear a man say to me, "You can't let me die until I have told my son I am sorry and to forgive me. I need to say I love him." To this day, I tell or maybe beg men to never be at the graveside talking to a dead father telling him you are sorry…forgive me, dad. There is that sacred place in us that we desire to express our love to our children. So, do it now, and don't let time catch up with you. If that time has passed, I will encourage you to visit a sacred place of remembrance as a symbolic act of love and forgiveness.

This secret, like life itself, ultimately resides within the heart of the God who created us. He knows what He is doing. It is no accident that we have the children we have. They are truly a gift from God. In His sovereignty, that means our Father can name them by name. What a gift of the Father. He did not give us the wrong kids, nor did he give them to the wrong man. That means that YOU are the only person whom he intends to father your children. Other men may stepfather your children, the schools may nurture your children, your wife may mother your children, and the government may foster your children, BUT only YOU can father YOUR children. YOU are the only one in possession of that secret that God wants to be implemented in the lives of YOUR children. We give ourselves to the grace of God. We do what we know He wants us to do, and we trust Him for the rest. We become devoted fathers who live by faith.

As we have concluded The Seven Secrets, your final job now is to evaluate yourself with our fathering profile at the end of the book. It will help you put into perspective our time together.

It is hard to "wind a book down to a final chapter." I said this would not be your typical book. Hopefully, you and I made some connections as you read it. As I say, "I bet we are a lot alike in our fathering story." The only difference is that I made a painful decision to expose my stories for one reason, and that is for you to feel free to talk about your stories. You and I and millions of other men across the world connect by being a father. Good, Bad, or Ugly, we are fathers. The question is, do you want to be an Effective Father? You may feel somewhat perplexed, confused, or have the feeling of being overwhelmed. But let me pull all this together in a pretty simple way.

Fatherhood can be summed up in One Word.
LOVE

Love manifests in three dimensions:

1. The intimate love between a husband and his wife
2. The protective love of parents for their children
3. The reaching out love of believers toward those who have no one else to love them—the orphans and widows.

What Works When All Else Fails?

God requires two simple steps: "If you confess your sins, He is faithful and just... to forgive you of your sins and to cleanse you from all unrighteousness." You and I must be sincere in that request. Not only does He forgive us, but He also cleanses both of us from all guilt and failure and restores us to pure conscience. The second requirement is to confess your sins to each other and pray for each other so God can heal you.

As you sit reading this took, you may have a feeling of failure. I would like to address that if you will read on with me. The Critical

Need is to Confess to those you've hurt. It is simple. You call out your wife's name or your child, and you simply say:

Kim, I love you. I am so sorry for the things I have done to hurt you.

Kim, Will you forgive me?

Brady and Casey, there is not an hour that goes by in my life that I regret what I said or did in your lives growing up. It is the biggest regret a father can have. Will you forgive me?

You may have the urge to speak of every hurt and trust me in saying that you will miss a bunch of hurts or some they have never voiced. The wording I just used is a great summary of the many ways men have tried to use.

I want you to hear from me that You Can Succeed!

Let me share how that happens: Take your Place as Head of Your family: Make that decision and commit. God will begin to build within your authority. You must trust God for the Grace you need: Being a Father is a calling of God just as sacred as being called to any religious job. I want you to hear that Mercy takes care of the Past and Grace for the Future.

In a broad sense, I gave you your father's job description in your toolbox. Go to it and open it up. I bet you find a tool you thought you had lost. I think the hard one for me, even though I knew deep down that my heart changed, was it will take some time. I just didn't become a bad dad or husband. You or I didn't just become a good dad. Words of hurt, regrets of the past, or violations of your marriage vows take some time for mercy, grace, love, and forgiveness to take the root of all the prior violations.

Let me address another small piece of advice. The walls of hurt might be high between you and your wife and kids that you regret. Remember when I said I had changed from that weekend event, but the warning was that just because you have changed does not mean your wife or your kids have changed. The walls may be high and fortified but if there is a mere shimmer of hope, then consider a counselor that can offer the skills of a referee and intercessor. I will admit it took me until the crisis was over to seek out a professional counselor. Why? Things got fixed. Things got better. It seems we won this "battle of the home," and it became OK.

But I found that I had to tend to some deeper wounds and consequences of my Little Boy Dave that remained hurt with the pain tucked away deep within my heart. As with a marriage partner, your wife's needs may need attention. There may be things she needs to deal with that affects you. It is not like whacking off the weed at the surface of the ground. The roots are still there. In time they will resurface. It was the very best gift I could ever give myself and our marriage. I encourage you to investigate that possibility. Let me just give you a warning that the small voice on your shoulder will try and convince you that it is all Ok now. You might want to gag that little voice.

Chapter 18
Final Thoughts

Do you remember my wish in the book's introduction? I wished that you and I could get away up in the mountains for a weekend talking about fathering. Imagine with me those two days of sharing our stories.

After we got settled in our house for the weekend, I sensed you were a bit anxious about what might happen with just the two of us with nowhere to run. Without saying anything, I knew the reality must have sunk in that it was just the two of us talking about some pretty sensitive issues with our marriages, kids, and life. I knew you realized it was too late to turn back. Still, I was pretty sure you realized you had placed yourself in a position of talking about some concerns in your life and family that weren't so good. I knew there you cared about being a good father because you said yes to the weekend. I knew I had to make it a safe place for you to feel OK to talk. I could feel you saying to yourself that you had made a mistake by coming on the trip and needed to go back home and just call it a bad idea. Then the reality would hit you of how you would explain it to your wife. I knew from the previous talks we had at the coffee shop that things hadn't gone quite the way you had imagined as a new groom on your wedding day, having all the dreams about being a great husband and father. I knew you had trusted me this far, and I couldn't let you down. Without a doubt, I knew I could share my hope for you, giving you the tools of being a better father and husband.

Final Thoughts

Like me at my weekend retreat, I sat quietly and listened. I made this internal vow that no one would hear what happens in my life or my home. My attitude was I was there, and then we will be done. As hours passed, I remember spending time trying to assure you that I know exactly how you feel, and I was proud you took me up on my offer, and we made the trip together.

I knew I would have to share a lot of my life as a failed father and husband for you to trust me and realize we all have a lot in common, and you weren't alone.

I just chose to talk about it to give you a pathway to tell your story. I kept assuring you that none of us wants to be a bad dad or husband. As I reminded you of a story, my goal was to identify my father wounds and reconcile them to move forward.

If you remember some of our first talks, I tried to let you feel and realize that we all fail and regret all the ugly stories we shared as husbands and fathers. I remember you looking at me a lot like I was this awful person. Soon, we took a break to gather up some wood for the fireplace during the night, and I looked over, and you were just staring at me. I asked you what's up? You got real tearful and said, "I have a lot in common with you, more than I wanted to admit, but too proud to say anything." I said, "I know, that was me." We had some tough conversations after supper before bed.

You started telling me your story about how you could never be good enough on the soccer pitch. All you could hear was your dad screaming at you when you missed the shot on goal. And grades became important to you in school because your dad wouldn't accept anything below an A because no good university would give you a scholarship. And there was the story where you got a girl pregnant your senior high school year, and your dad told you to "take care of it." I watched you begin to sob almost uncontrollably, telling me the story of taking your girlfriend for an abortion. You said you still have nightmares about the son or daughter you never knew. I remember you just sitting there telling me how you felt sick to your stomach about being any kind of father or husband. How could you be either when you aborted a child. Boy, could I identify with that from the nights in that hotel during my fathering course—all I could do was lay there on the floor and cry. Like you, I didn't think I could move forward with anything in life with so much pain and failure.

I just knew in our talks this time had to be more than just sharing ugly stories but getting into the toolbox. Like me, I was sick of my story and needed to hear how to move forward with more than just drinking coffee, talking about the same stuff. I realized that he was ready to open the toolbox and learn how to use the tools or secrets. So, I opened up the box.

The minutes turned into hours. As we talked, I was thrilled watching him pick up a tool and examine it and want to know more about how to use it. It got late at night, and we knew it was time to call it a day. We made our way to our bedrooms, and the house was suddenly silent except for the crackling of the fire. As I started to drift off to sleep, I ask God to reveal to you the very nature of Fatherhood. I remember saying to God, "Father, would you heal the scars of the little boy, so he awakes fresh and renewed?" Would you do that, God? Then I found myself drifting off to sleep, thinking how God can just quietly and gently touch the hurts of our lives and make us whole." As Kim says, "God knows."

We woke up on the second day and fixed some hot coffee sitting out on the house's front porch. The air had a crisp feel to it, and life seemed like the world was sitting still. It went without saying that I think we wished we didn't have to go back to the city. After a lot of silence, I ask you what you had come up with so far about your fathering and marriage. What could we conclude so far? After we talked some more about the Seven Secrets and identified some of our tools, it was a lot to absorb. I was hoping you would be direct and straight about things in your life and not just say what you thought I might want to hear. Were you going to be different in facing your past failures? I know I was dead honest, telling you all about my mess. I was glad when you started talking about how inconsistent you had been at home and that looking back at things, no one had really talked to you about how to listen to your kids and to pray for them by name as a spiritual father.

We stopped for a short lunch and kept talking. We had been talking about how we might better demonstrate love to our family. It seemed we kept coming back to forgiveness and reconciliation and how we can't move forward in our family without sitting down and dealing with those issues. I seemed to sense that the more we talked, there was a hope of transforming your thinking about yourself and hoping your family would extend mercy and grace for all the things you didn't do well.

Toward the late afternoon, we knew time was approaching to head home. As we sat on the porch, I wondered if you really took things seriously and reflected on your life as a son and now as a father. I wondered if you explored places in your life that harbor pain and hurt. We sat for a few more minutes, and I ask if you remembered our conversations about all the things that caused hurt and how to find those opportunities to walk in health and new life. In that, I ask you when your last medical physical was where you got a thorough examination. You just laughed at me and said Never, and you said you didn't even have a doctor. We just started laughing after I started walking out in front of the house, squawking like a chicken saying, this is how you look. I said you're really a big chicken.

The time had come to load up and begin our trip back home to face all the realities of home, work, and being a husband and father. It made me wish that men would take a time-out in life just for a few days to get a fresh look at their marriages and themselves as fathers. I had hoped our time together was as good for you as me.

As the trip home seemed to go fast, we pulled over for gas in this small country store with a couple of old gas pumps. While sitting in the car watching you pump gas in the car, I got to thinking again about the two days in the mountains. I was hoping you heard my challenge for you to ask yourself that if we were at all similar, do you think you stuck away all the things that had hurt you and lost track of them?

Somewhere in our discussions, I mentioned that I finally had to come to grips that I needed to admit some ugly things about my life as a father and husband. As we talked, I shared that my path to uncovering those unmarked graves of hurt came with an incredible counselor. She gently walked me to those doors and helped me open them safely and with caution. With her careful navigation, I got them open and dealt with them. We challenged ourselves to go back and look at the men in our families that experienced hurts, disappointments, and unhealthy family behaviors that pass from one generation of men to others. We decided these negative behaviors had to stop with us. As with me, I learned I just couldn't "will" my hurts to go away or not continue to talk about them.

Suddenly, the car door opened, and you asked me if everything was OK as I seemed to be staring into space. I said, "Yeah, I was just thinking about our time together, reflecting on my stories, and they made me think about some things again." You asked me what was going on, and I said I was just asking myself some of the questions we talked about up in the mountains." You asked me, "what were they?" I said I was just asking myself if I was still the leader of my family as I first desired? Was I still taking responsibility to lead and direct my family? Am I healthy spiritually, emotionally, and psychologically and ever-present? Or had I got relaxed and took things for granted and assumed everything was just fine, never asking the questions if things were still good.

I guess I asked myself the same question again because I challenge leaders everywhere I travel and teach. The basic premise is that we cannot effectively lead congregations, corporations, or a family business behind a mask of hurt, fragility, and brokenness. Leading behind a mask will catch up with you sooner or later. It will either be a failed career, financial failures, broken family, or marriage with fractured kid relationships. I wish I had a dollar for every man I bought lunch who called himself the leader. They had lost a marriage through a divorce, inter-office affair, fractured kid relationship, or his health over a business. While climbing to be that person, you look up one day and find out what you lost in your life. These men lost their toolbox along the way if there were ever one. I sort of had some semblance of one, and thankfully I found it before it was too late. I am really conscious about those questions for myself because I was the leader behind the mask.

We kept driving, and it seemed there were long miles without many conversations between us. My mind drifted off, and I got to thinking about the friends that "came to my rescue." They were men I would generally not drink coffee with because they seemed to be the perfect husband and have perfect kids. I mean, I just didn't have much in common. I referred to them as the "Ken and Barbie." If those same guys sat with me again, I would congratulate them on being good dads and how they seemed to do it right. I think I would tell them they can now deal more effectively with the guy in the breakroom or Sunday School class that just "threw up on him about his kid," and he is looking for help. Now, these guys will have a lot to share based on truth, facts based on the Seven Secrets, and not emotional or personal opinions. What a great opportunity for them to share a tool from their toolbox. Good for them.

We drove into a small town and pulled up to a red-light. I turned and asked, "how will you see things differently about your family when you get home?" We talked about making life or fathering behavioral changes that affect our relationship with our children. We discovered, there is no magic bullet. On the positive side, we discovered we had many tools in our toolbox that worked well, and some were breaking and needed replacement. Hopefully, we discovered that we are not alone in lacking the tools to be effective fathers and warm and loving husbands. At that red light, I think you finally jumped over that big hurdle when you said, "I hope my wife forgives me when we sit down and talk about the weekend." That is when I felt you knew it was going to more time than you ever expected. You looked at me and said, "Clark, do you realize that I really didn't have a clue what I was supposed to be or how to act as a husband or father? I had no idea about these tools you kept referring to as we talked, but I will be buying a toolbox tomorrow." We laughed and drove off.

I remember driving out of that town, telling him to be sure and have that mental checklist we had discussed the things requiring attention. You asked me for the first time if I had one? I remember saying, "absolutely." You asked me if I would tell you what was number one on the list? I remember saying that my checklist had gone all over the place over the past years. Right now, the top issue is constantly asking myself how much I love my wife and kids, and did my behavior represent that? Odd question, but as I said, we still harbor things that cause us to still hurt those we love the most when it is not our desire. I still have to keep that one on the list to watch each day. I told you I knew you deeply love your wife and children because you had taken time to stop life with me and try to get a new start with your wife and kids. I told you I never stopped my love for my family, but I had to stop some old behavior playing out in my head and heart. I told you we all wish differently, even though many, if not most of us, were raised in decent families. Somewhere along the way, we discovered we had difficulty extending the love like God designed. Things just went wrong. And for the life of us, we couldn't seem to point our finger at it.

As we drove into town and you pulled up to my house to let me out before you drove home, I looked at you, hoping this would not just be a weekend we soon forget. Looking at my house reminded me of when I came home from my weekend retreat. I was renewed and refreshed but scared to death about what would happen next. Before I got out of your car, I had a dozen thoughts about what to say to you. Of all the things I could have said to you, I only made one comment, "I hope you say Yes." I was hoping you would be brave and challenge yourself to make that one big decision that would cause the rest of your changes to take place. As we had been together all weekend, I thought it would have been a perfect time, but I had to remember how long it took for me to say that word. As I shut my car door, I hollered at you and said, "Hey, don't shut out friends, and you know I will always buy you that cup of coffee. Be brave."

While walking up to my porch after you drove off from my house, I wondered what reception you would receive from your wife and kids? After all, we both had changed over that weekend, but those who await us have not.

Was your homecoming going to be like mine, where Kim could have cared less about what happened over the weekend?

When I came into my house, Kim greeted me and asked how were the two days in the mountains and how was I? She knows me well, as each time that I teach or visit with men, it still has a profound impact on me and brings me into a new awareness of the depth of my Fatherhood. It seems always to open a door I thought had opened. As we settled in, she asked what was going on with me? As we talked over the weekend, I had this deeper awareness of how our past hurts us as a child or husband and the impact on fathering behaviors. I always talk about legacy, pain, shame, forgiveness, reconciliation, and the little boy that acts his pain out as an adult boy. I realized when I teach that I don't talk enough about some of the basic fathering foundations that guide our behavior.

I have spent a lot of time writing about a man's relationship with his Father and the lifelong impact of his behavior with his children. I often write, "if I could do it over again," as my way of saying, "I really messed up," and wished I had years back in raising my boys. Men tell me all the time, "Yeah, Clark, that is just normal for all of us. You're too hard on yourself." While there is some truth to this, I feel my burden goes much deeper. I think I have seen the eyes of too many boys and girls wounded by a dad who was clueless he just hurt this little heart with their toxic words or a hard jerk of their arms in front of their friends. It is like watching a fragile glass just crack before my eyes. I must admit my emotions fly from wanting to "hit him" or grab the kids and hold them to say he didn't really want to do that.

One thing I have realized over the years is that our past relationship with our dads continues in our adulthood. As my story revealed, words in my childhood and my family were powerful, or maybe I should say many times stinging and harsh. Words matter and we need to realize we get trained by our words. Words ripple through our lives, shaping our behavior as a child and into adulthood. It affects our wholeness of who we are in life. A good definition of wholeness is when the way of our being matches the truth of our being and how that integrates with God. That brings up the question of what is the truth of your being? Will the real Dave Clark stand up?

As we learned in The Course, television and childhood friends influence our kids' lives than our family. We have learned that men are degraded and ridiculed by television shows and have been objects of jokes. Certainly, the feminist movements across the world have minimized the importance of men. Now we can change our sexual preference, and gay couples are no longer hidden in the closet and can be parents of children. Men have inertly assumed feelings of worthlessness. I find shame and worthlessness are tie-breakers for men with their self-image and how they act out of those emotions in their lives.

Here is a good thought. If you don't know the truth of your being is anything good, then you're going to lead your life as an expression of what you believe is the truth. Let me put it this way, "If you think you are worthless or deprived – don't be surprised if your life takes on those characteristics." Whatever you think in your heart is whom you portray.

What that means is that I tried to present myself to others as a good father or husband when I was faking it. I try to put on characteristics of being OK when I am really covering up that I am a piece of crap. It means those ugly things that have made me feel shameful, deplorable, worthless, or taught to me have been hidden. It goes so far as to believe that we believe God thinks I am hopeless, and it drives me down into the ground. After all, what we think about ourselves is who we are. If you believe that your God created everything as good on earth – then something has to be good before it is broken. Read that again.

The truth of the matter is we are a good creation of who we are and worthy of being loved, which is more fundamental than any of the damage that occurred in your life. We have just lost sight of it over time, or we have believed the words of others or our deep unhealthy voices who say we are worthless.

It is like a building block. Our basic foundation is goodness. But over time, other blocks are placed on our foundation. In most cases, it causes us to lose sight of our initial foundation of goodness. That is where we need to refocus our thinking and visualization. We forget our basic foundation, and in this case, it is goodness. No matter our faith, the foundational basis in creation is Good.

Let's look again at our relationship with our dads. Again, I will say I am not making our dads as bad guys. However, we have to agree that our good and bad personality formation derives a lot from his behavior. I will go back to my dad coming at me with a belt that night when I was afraid to go into a dark house with my little brother. First, he verbally humiliated me, taking me to each room, turning on the lights asking me where the ghosts were in each room. Then came the belt and fury and what comes out of my mouth and thousand of little boys and girls when they are in trouble, three words: "I'll Be Good!" Daddy, don't hit me, "I'll Be Good!" Daddy, "If you would just give me one more chance." "I will do better!" In other words, I will do better to win your affection and approval. Now, put that in perspective with our relationship with God. We keep "rededicating ourselves to God" at the front of the church, and we keep repenting about the same ole' stuff. We keep trying to produce righteousness based on self-discipline and performance, which literally drives us into the bad. If I have failed as a father, I keep piling on stuff to be better, not believing the fundamental truth I am already good.

The issue then becomes of who we are in the Father. Certainly, the Father sees us as his good and worthy children. One issue is overcoming toxic thoughts and behavior that we are not a good person. How on earth could I be a good husband and father with all I have done to my kids and wife? We could just say "enough, I'm done" or just jump out of a moving car in total desperation.

Let's talk about Kim at this point. Remember her story? When you get beat up verbally and when you seem to stand up that you only seem to get kicked down. What happened to Kim? She said, "I'm done." She turned off her emotions and slipped into her own darkness, and everything of value hit the toilet. People ask us every conference, "what happened?" We both will give the basic response that when Dave changed, our family begin (slowly) to trust this new guy or, as Kim said, the guy I once fell in love with and married. Let me add a footnote to this: As a team, we fail and win. However, the leader of the family is you, men. Go back and re-read Kim's chapter.

I find in most cases that even in the depth of darkness is always the man that knows there is a faint light and can barely see it, but he sees the light of what we call goodness. When I sit with a man who is at his end, I ask him does he see any light. He may quickly say, "NO." It is when I ask him the second or third time to look again, and he will say, "Yeah, I think I see it." You see a faint of hope re-emerge.

When the message is driven into a man's head by his father, his wife, and even his grown children that he is a worthless father, that man will walk away from the light as glowing as it may be. He is unable to visualize that he is anything but what they labeled him. He will keep reading his books on fathering or go to a fathering class (rededicating himself to Fatherhood) or a church men's retreat. He may find no one helps him find his way back to his foundation, finding the cracks and flaws and resolving them, not piling on super glue. The ugly picture is this guy is whom I described earlier in the book. This man was the guy sitting in the coffee shop in total personal and family desperation or maybe destruction, looking for answers, or what I call trying to reach the light. He desperately tries to Say Yes but can't get the words out because he doesn't feel good enough for God.

I think this is where fathers save fathers. I wrote this book as much for the good Father as the dad who needs to find his fatherhood toolbox. You see, the man who has finally found his light or has figured out how to get past the disfigured blocks of his foundation and find his original foundation of GOOD is that he has his hope. He is now better positioned to share his story and share a solid toolbox that is not generalized opinions or just his story. I remember a man telling me after I shared my story at a conference that he had thought about attending one of my fatherhood courses. In a funny way, he said, "Clark, if I have to go through what you did, I don't want anything to do with it."

You see, the story (like the pastor's sermon) is important, but at the end of the story or sermon, somebody better give me the "how." The toolbox is the how.

Don't be fooled. This intervention does not require a pastor or some spiritual leader. The everyday father that has come to grip with his fatherhood is the perfect navigator. In other words, our goal is to navigate a man to Say Yes. He is saying Yes to being whole and realize his goodness. He is saying Yes to discard negative messages that, over time, bombarded his foundation of goodness that seemingly vanished. When we accomplish the reality of being good and not bad, the messages become clearer. We truly become effective as a man, husband, and father. So, guys, the deeper challenge is not just sit in a fathering class or attend some warm and fuzzy men's conference only to fall on our faces months later. I call those things (as good as they seem) adding on (or re-dedicating our fatherhood time again) when we have failed to go to the basic foundation of goodness and believe it. We can't keep adding on things to an already unhealthy foundation.

Can I tell you one last story? It is the story of the Prodigal Son. You may want to go back and refresh your memory (it's in the Christian Bible). I am going to tell you the short version of the story. It goes something like this: You see, when the Prodigal Son returned home in shame and dishonor from wanting to go out and live life and be his own self-made man, he would have been content if his father had simply let him be a servant within the household. Yet not only did the prodigal son regain his dignity of sonship, but his father provided a special meal to celebrate his restoration. Meals in that time were special for creating and renewing covenant bonds among friends and family members. Let's remember that the word covenant can mean a binding or contractual relationship between two parties. The father's feast was the pinnacle of the prodigal's restored sonship. Sharing his father's meal meant the prodigal's restored sonship. Sharing his father's meal meant the prodigal shared again in his father's covenant life. At this table, the formerly estranged son and father became one.

It is from this restored covenant relationship with God that we discover the heart of our Fatherhood. Out of the abundance of our divine sonship, we discover the strength to become the type of father God intends for us: earthly fathers reflecting our children the image of "our Father." Be strong and say Yes to this covenant relationship.

You see, we have this beautiful development of the very being of the Father within us – You have God, the Father. You have the Father, who is a father in every one of us whether we want to declare it or not. We can argue this, debate it, deny it, but the very truth of the matter is the Father is in every one of us. Every male or female is his sons and daughters. What the father does is open up a path so our kids know the truth of their being. It is sort of like that Eighth Secret we discussed. There are these undefinable moments that warm our hearts and stirs the very foundation of our deepest feelings. Guys, this is the source. We are the sons. We are to call him Abba, which means I am his little boy. There is something in us that knows what it is like to desire to be small and protected by a great father – many of us didn't have a father or have a relationship to experience these moments. I can assure you this God, this Father has this desire to have this relationship with his sons and daughters. There is in all of us this enact capacity to believe and receive a really wonderful father even if we didn't have one or experience this relationship with him. It is available to all of us. This is the Yes I desire you to speak out to Him.

Right now, you are in either two places with me in the final paragraphs of this book. The first is you are ready to make some changes and risk the Yes to a new life as a husband and a father. In saying this, you receive so many things, but perhaps the biggest prize is regaining your wholeness in your family. My comment to men all over the world may sound a bit sarcastic. But I say it anyway. Why? Because we are at the edge of a canyon with two distinct scenarios: The first is that in saying Yes to a change, you will be looking at a new sunrise in your life. What seems like barren rocks, cliffs, rugged and jagged pastures with snakes and scorpions turns into a beauty of the sun reflecting off the land to a distinct beauty unlike any you have seen. The second place is if you say NO, you are on the edge of nothingness. There are no reflections of the sun magnifying creation. At the end of the day is the failure of unhappiness and another taste of failure.

I thought that was a pertinent story for our last chapter and have a good word picture. To the one reading this story, I wanted to say how I enjoyed sharing my life with you. It has taken me more than three years to finish this book between my dad's death and my wife's father and other family members, including my mom. Men worldwide have asked me if I had a book about my story of the Seven Secrets. As my wife and I retired from work, we knew the time was right to share the details of The Father's Cry. My wife, Kim, traveled with me on our last trip to Pakistan to train more fatherhood trainers. I remember when we sat in the Lahore, Pakistan airport, she asked me about the book. I remember telling her I just couldn't emotionally pick it back up with my dad dying. For several years, I saw the book icon on my computer desktop, and I just kept scrolling past it. Finally, one day, I stared at it for what seemed like hours and found my right hand clicking the file open

I realized the time had come two years after his death that I could get words on a keyboard again. Toward the end of his life, we talked freely about death, heaven, faith, family, and his legacy to his sons and our family. My dad had deeply embedded the voices of his past and present. Many of those voices were living out in our lives. Some voices were good and bad. As his sons, we have worked hard to recognize those inner voices that hurt us and those that helped us. He knew the things that had hurt his three sons in the later years of his life. We saw sweetness, gentleness, and love evolve with the need for us to forgive him, and we did. Yet, even in his late years of life, there were times a quick temper would stir up, but my mom was quick to say, "Clark, you don't need to talk that way anymore." And like a door slammed, he would immediately stop. My dad never sat in a fatherhood course. He never took a class on fathering. It was later in his life that he attended a conference with me and sat in the back of the room. I remember on the drive home, we stopped at a red light.

We hadn't said anything from the conference parking lot till the second or third red light. Then out it came. I am sorry. Fighting back my tears at the red light, all I could say is 'it was OK.' His toolbox had some broken tools in it. Over time, those broken tools vanished. We got the benefit of burying a man who left a positive legacy for his family. I think at the end of the day that all three sons got a pretty good toolbox. Not perfect, dents, chipped paint, and maybe a few tools that never found their way to the box. Dad had forgiven himself for all the things that lived out in our home as little boys and teenagers.

As I wrote this book, I remembered in the later years of my career traveling across Texas. My dad would always call me and ask me where I was going or what town and hospital I was heading for the week. Every single time before we would end the call, he would tell me he loved me. I am in my seventies. As my brothers and I would sit and talk during the times his health deteriorated, we all figured out he was calling each of us every week or so to say, "where are you, come home before it gets too dark." We seldom heard those words as kids, but they brought smiles to our faces. I realized even writing these stories that my dad continued to demonstrate being a husband taking care of my mom, who was in a wheelchair till her death. He tended to her every need. In retrospect, I think he even showed us how to die.

It was early in the morning, and my phone rang at home. I was supposed to go pick up my dad from the nursing home to go to a grandson's house for Easter. It was the Emergency Room nurse at the hospital, and they said my dad was admitted and not doing well. It wasn't the first alarm with my dad, but I sensed this was not right. The nursing home didn't call but the Emergency Room. It was 5:00 a.m. As I walked into the hospital's Emergency Department, I was once the Senior Vice-President was a familiar nurse's face. They had placed dad on a breathing machine to help him breathe. She had remembered my dad and our wishes not to prolong his life at his age. She looked right at me and said, "you want to take this off of him, don't you." I said yes, knowing this was the last trip to the hospital. I called my two brothers and said, "you need to get here," and they both caught a plane together and arrived in hours. We called the Hospice team, and while we were waiting, my two brothers were at his bedside. I remember in his last hours when he whispered toward Steve, "Am I dying?" And my big brother leaned over to him lovingly and tenderly said, "Yes." My dad gently laid his head back on the pillow as to say OK and later died. I knew we three had come full circle with our dad as we loved him and had the incredible and lifelong honor of ushering him to be with his Father.

My dad saw the need to forgive himself and us forgive him. My dad was always teaching each of his sons how to be a husband and father, or I should say, a better man. My dad saw his job as preparing us for life and not to be a failure but to be the best. It took him until later in life to realize he missed the connection of nurturing us. He never saw that as part of being a father. He never quit teaching us, from showing us how to detail cars or mow a yard to the need to check on his kids each week. I am glad my dad found his hidden voices, dealt with his demons, and understood the need to leave a positive legacy. Toward his end, my dad broke a lot of bad generational habits. My dad came through as a different man. I forgave him many times over the end of his life. I realized over his later years of transformation and forgiveness what he had been teaching me. Maybe in hindsight, dad had dug through his many foundations of toxic behavior and generational stigmas and saw the light he knew was always there. My dad knew what was good, but so many other persuasive things seem to detour him. Why would I say that? I watched a man deal with bad behavior, regrets, bad habits, and maybe a toolbox that had a bunch of missing tools that he tried to figure out how they work. I know he didn't keep piling on one bad foundation on top of the other because we all witnessed my dad systematically tear into his past as to make it right.

Early on, I think I missed a lot of what my dad was trying to say to me. I had been so much a part of his forgiveness and so wrapped up with the effect on my life that I missed a more significant part of his message: "Dave, this is how you do it. Just don't wait as long as I did and take your family through years of turmoil to learn a hard lesson like me." My thoughts many times were, "Dad, you could have just said it." But I had to remember, that was not how men were programed in his generation. In hindsight, I think that was part of him breaking or stopping those generation habits for us to be different and learn. As I tell men across the world, "never let your kids doubt how much you love them. You have to tell them." At his death, all three brothers stood at his grave and could say, "Dad, you finished well. We are proud to call you, dad."

Before the ending paragraph, let me warmly wish you the best at being an effective father and husband. It is your destiny. You are great.

Final Thoughts

You are worthy. Your foundation is good. You are precisely who God created you to be.

As odd as it seems, I am ending the book with a quote from my youngest son from the Foreword introducing this book. It was his last paragraph and fittingly so the last paragraph of this book:

> *"I now feel that there is nothing that would separate me from the love of my parents. This, I think, is a commendable example of God's love, The Love. I think it could have easily gone the other way. I mean, the disconnect could still be there, like it is for a lot of families. But the message of hope is this: Our family was hopeless, and here I am writing about how it worked out, despite our low points. Not that there won't be new low points as the next Clark generation emerges, but by the pure grace of God, it will be built on a strong foundation."*

Casey Clark, Son, and Member of The Father's Cry Ministry
** 7 Secrets Profile PDF**

THE IMPACT OF FATHERLESSNESS ON CHILDREN

Children with involved Fathers are more confident, better able to deal with frustration, better able to gain independence and their own identity, more likely to mature into compassionate adults, more likely to have high self-esteem, more sociable, more secure as infants, less likely to show signs of depression, less likely to commit suicide, more empathetic, boys have been shown to be less aggressive and adolescent girls are less likely to engage in sex.

1. Effects on Fatherlessness
   - 85% of all children that exhibit behavioral disorders come from fatherless homes
   - 90% of all homeless and runaway children are from fatherless homes
   - 71% of all high school dropouts come from fatherless homes
   - 75% of all adolescent patients in chemical abuse centers come from fatherless homes
   - 63% of youth suicides are from fatherless homes
   - Juvenile Delinquency/ Crime/ Gangs
   - 80% of rapists motivated with displaced anger come from fatherless homes
   - 70% of juveniles in state-operated institutions come from fatherless homes
   - 85% of all youths sitting in prisons grew up in a fatherless home

2. Impact of Children from a Fatherless Home
   - 5 times more likely to commit suicide
   - 32 times more likely to run away
   - 20 times more likely to have behavioral disorders
   - 14 times more likely to commit rape
   - 9 times more likely to drop out of high school
   - 10 times more likely to abuse chemical substances
   - 9 times more likely to end up in a state-operated institution
   - 20 times more likely to end up in prison

3. Teenage Pregnancy
    - Daughters of single parents are 53% more likely to marry as teenagers, 164% more likely to have a premarital birth, and 92% more likely to dissolve their own marriages.
    - 71% of teenage pregnancies are to children of single parents.

THE 7 SECRETS PROFILE

INSTRUCTIONS:

Decide how accurate the following statements are concerning your fathering practices. Circle the appropriate answer beside each statement. If your children are no longer living in your home, respond as you remember when they were at home. If your children are very young, think ahead to what you will do based on the experience you've already had with your children. If you are not a father, answer the questions based on your experience with your own father while growing up.

FATHERING DIMENSIONS:

**1 = MOSTLY FALSE   2 = SOMEWHAT FALSE   3 = UNDECIDED
4 = SOMEWHAT TRUE   5 = MOSTLY TRUE**

FD1. I avoid action in fathering my children.	1 2 3 4 5
FD2. I have a good handle on how my child's needs change as he/she grows up.	1 2 3 4 5
FD3. My moods are pretty much the same from day to day.	1 2 3 4 5
FD4. I pay attention to my children when they speak to me.	1 2 3 4 5
FD5. I tend to delay doing the things I know I should do as a father.	1 2 3 4 5
FD6. I feel that the way I deal with my children does not change much from day to day.	1 2 3 4 5
FD7. I carefully listen to my children express their concerns.	1 2 3 4 5
FD8. I know what my child needs in order to grow into a mature, responsible person.	1 2 3 4 5
FD9. I have difficulty in being motivated to do my fathering tasks.	1 2 3 4 5

© 2006 National Center for Fathering

FD10. I do not change much in the way that I deal with my children. 1 2 3 4 5

FD11. It is hard for me to get going in my fathering role. 1 2 3 4 5

FD12. I know what is reasonable to expect from my children for their age. 1 2 3 4 5

FD13. I listen to my children when they talk to me. 1 2 3 4 5

FD14. I do not have major shifts in my moods. 1 2 3 4 5

FD15. I rarely have time to play games with my children. 1 2 3 4 5

FD12. I know what is reasonable to expect from my children for their age. 1 2 3 4 5

FD13. I listen to my children when they talk to me. 1 2 3 4 5

FD14. I do not have major shifts in my moods. 1 2 3 4 5

FD15. I rarely have time to play games with my children. 1 2 3 4 5

FD15. I rarely have time to play games with my children. 1 2 3 4 5

FD16. I know my child's growth needs. 1 2 3 4 5

FD17. I am predictable in the way I relate to my children. 1 2 3 4 5

FD18. My children and I seldom have time to work together. 1 2 3 4 5

FD19. I show my children that I care when they share a problem with me. 1 2 3 4 5

FD20. I know what motivates my child. 1 2 3 4 5

FD21. I tend to be somewhat unchanging in the way I practice fathering responsibilities. 1 2 3 4 5

FD22. I rarely spend time with my children. 1 2 3 4 5

© 2006 National Center for Fathering

FATHERING PRACTICES:

**1 = VERY POOR 2 = POOR 3 = FAIR
4 = GOOD 5 = VERY GOOD**

FP1. Being "level-headed" during a crisis.　　　　　　　　　1 2 3 4 5

FP2. Being romantic with my wife.　　　　　　　　　　　　1 2 3 4 5

FP3. Reading spiritually-oriented material with my children often.　1 2 3 4 5

FP4. Knowing what to do in a family crisis.　　　　　　　　1 2 3 4 5

FP5. Spending time with my wife away from the children.　　1 2 3 4 5

FP6. Praying with my children.　　　　　　　　　　　　　1 2 3 4 5

FP7. Being able to deal with a crisis in a positive manner.　　1 2 3 4 5

FP8. Knowing what my children are able to do for their age.　1 2 3 4 5

FP9. Handling crisis in a mature manner.　　　　　　　　　1 2 3 4 5

FP10. Having a good relationship with my wife.　　　　　　1 2 3 4 5

FP11. Having a family worship time in the home.　　　　　　1 2 3 4 5

FP12. Having a steady income.　　　　　　　　　　　　　1 2 3 4 5

FP13. Discussing my children's development with my wife.　1 2 3 4 5

FP14. Knowing the issues with which my children are dealing.　1 2 3 4 5

FP15. Talking about spiritual things with my children.　　　1 2 3 4 5

FP16. Having a job that provides adequate income for my family.　1 2 3 4 5

FP17. Discussing my children's problems with my wife.　　1 2 3 4 5

FP18. Stressing the importance of spiritual values with my family.　1 2 3 4 5

FP19. Providing for the basic needs of my family.　　　　　1 2 3 4 5

SECRET #2: Effective fathers know their children

FD2 Score _____ I have a good handle on how my child's need change as he/she grows up.

FD8 Score _____ I know what my child needs in order to grow into a mature responsible person.

FD12 Score _____ I know what is reasonable to expect from my children for their age.

FD16 Score _____ I know my children's growth needs.

FD20 Score _____ I know what motivates my child.

FP8 Score _____ Knowing what my children are able to do for their age.

FP14 Score _____ Knowing the issues with which my children are dealing.

TOTAL _____

Plot Your Score:

7 9 11 13 15 17 19 21 23 25 27 29 31 33 35

SECRET #3: Effective fathers are consistent

FD3 Score _____ My moods are pretty much the same from day to day.

FD6 Score _____ I feel that the way I deal with my children does not change much from day to day.

FD10 Score _____ I do not change much in the way that I deal with my children.

FD14 Score _____ I do not have major shifts in my moods.

FD17 Score _____ I am predictable in the way that I relate to my children.

FD21 Score _____ I tend to be somewhat unchanging in the way I practice fathering responsibilities.

TOTAL _____

Plot Your Score:

6 8 10 12 14 16 18 20 22 24 26 28 30

SECRET #4:
Effective fathers protect and provide for their children

FP1 Score _____ Being "level-headed" during a crisis.

FP4 Score _____ Knowing what to do in a family crisis.

FP7 Score _____ Being able to deal with crisis in a positive manner.

FP9 Score _____ Handling crisis in a mature manner.

FP12 Score _____ Having a steady income.

FP16 Score _____ Having a job that provides adequate income for my family.

FP19 Score _____ Providing for the basic needs of my family.

Plot Your Score:

| 7 | 9 | 11 | 13 | 15 | 17 | 19 | 21 | 23 | 25 | 27 | 29 | 31 | 33 | 35 |

SECRET #5:
Effective fathers love their children's mother

FP2 Score _____ Being romantic with my wife.

FP5 Score _____ Spending time with my wife away from my children.

FP10 Score _____ Having a good relationship with my wife.

FP13 Score _____ Discussing my children's development with my wife.

FP17 Score _____ Discussing my children's problems with my wife.

TOTAL _____

Plot Your Score:

| 5 | 7 | 9 | 11 | 13 | 15 | 17 | 19 | 21 | 23 | 25 |

© 2006 National Center for Fathering

SECRET #6:
Effective fathers are active listeners to their children

FD4 Score ____ I pay attention to my children when they speak to me.

FD7 Score ____ I carefully listen to my children express their concerns.

FD13 Score ____ I listen to my children when they talk to me.

FD19 Score ____ I show my children that I care when they share a problem with me.

TOTAL ____

Plot Your Score:

4   6   8   10   12   14   16   18   20

SECRET #7:
Effective fathers spiritually equip their children

FP3 Score ____ Reading spiritually-oriented material with my children often.

FP6 Score ____ Praying with my children.

FP11 Score ____ Having a family worship time in the home.

FP15 Score ____ Talking about spiritual things with my children.

FP18 Score ____ Stressing the importance of spiritual values with my family.

TOTAL ____

Plot Your Score:

5   7   9   11   13   15   17   19   21   23   25

© 2006 National Center for Fathering

THE 7 SECRETS PROFILE: SUMMARY

INSTRUCTIONS:

Transfer the scores from each of the secrets to the corresponding scales on the last page of this scoring profile to identify your specific strengths and areas that "need work." The scales are not uniform because they are based on norms from a study group of 1,650 fathers.

INTERPRETING THE RESULTS:

The 7 Secrets Profile has been designed to help fathers obtain feedback on their approach to fathering. Recognize that fathering is a creative, complex and challenging occupation. It has many aspects and requires different approaches for different circum-stances and conditions.

Be easy on yourself as you review your results. The Profile is limited. It cannot assess your heart, your desire. It can only give you a reference point about your relationship with your children. The Profile is a tool that can assist you in evaluating your fathering practices for the purpose of planning ways to modify and strengthen areas as you desire.

There are some things that you do better than others — your strengths. Don't short-change yourself. Don't say, "I have no strengths." Review your Profile and note your strengths in the space below. Rejoice and capitalize on your strengths. Don't forget them.

There are other areas where you have opportunity for improvement. Note them in the space below. You need to work on these. But don't try to apply yourself to all of these at once. Pick one — maybe two — areas that you want to strengthen, and focus your efforts there. Review your seminar notes and the chapters in the 7 Secrets book and begin your improvement work with the help of other men.

© 2006 National Center for Fathering

Remember, this is a snapshot of where you are today. With a firm commitment and a good plan, you can improve your fathering and become the dad you want to be.

MY STRENGTHS ARE:

MY OPPORTUNITIES ARE:

PERSONAL ACTION PLAN:

Secret	Low			Average		High
SECRET #1: Effective fathers are committed to their children.	35	29	22	16	11	7
SECRET #2: Effective fathers know their children.	7	14	22	27	31	35
SECRET #3: Effective fathers are consistent in their attitudes and behavior.	6	12	18	23	27	30
SECRET #4: Effective fathers pro-tect and provide for their children.	7	16	26	30	33	35
SECRET #5: Effective fathers love their children's mother.	5	11	16	19	22	25
SECRET #6: Effective fathers are active listeners to their children.	4	9	14	17	19	20
SECRET #7: Effective fathers spiritually equip their children.	5	9	12	16	21	25

© 2006 *National Center for Fathering*

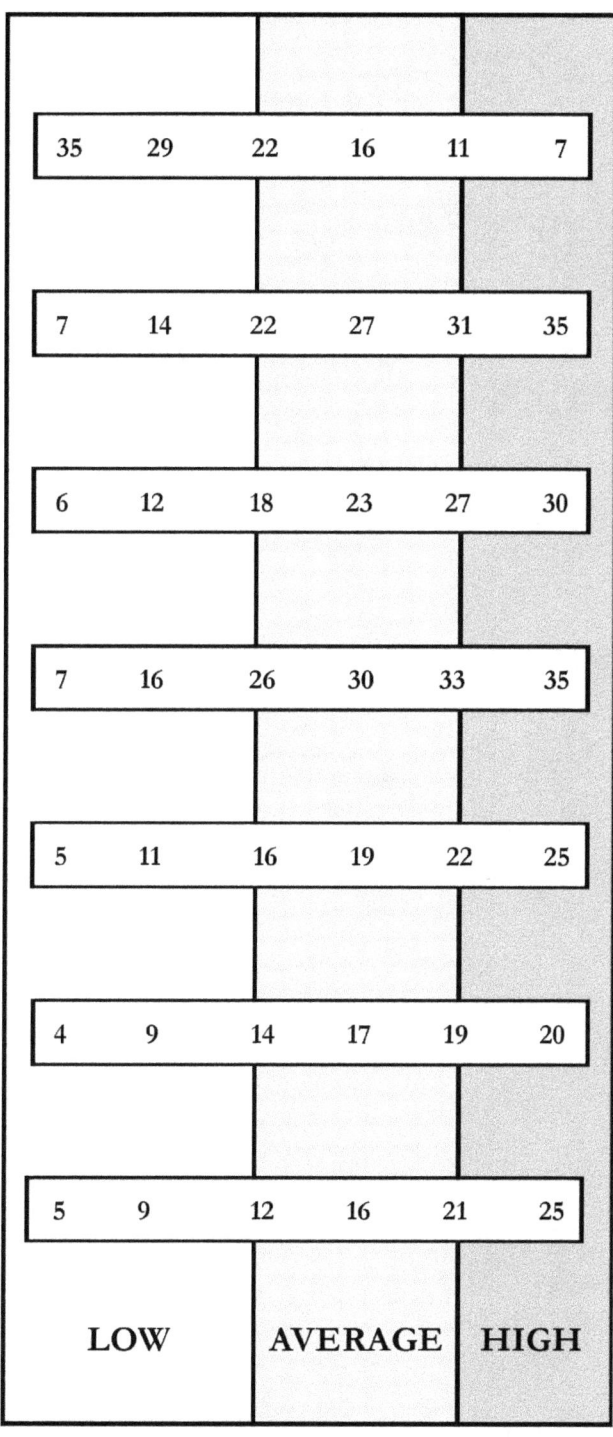

Dave Clark is the President of The Father's Cry, an international fathering ministry (www.thefatherscry.org). Dave is a retired healthcare consultant working in the medical profession for over fifty years. He is married to Kim since 1975 with two grown sons, Braden and Casey.

The Clark family established fatherhood programs throughout the United States, Eastern Africa, South Africa, United Arab Emirates, and Pakistan. Dave speaks at men's conferences, schools, prisons, clubs, civic organizations, and churches, along with his wife, Kim, and his two sons. Dave is a Master Trainer for the National Center for Fathering. While experiencing personal tragedy and family devastation with a son who chose gangs, drugs, weapons, and jail, Dave gives a fresh approach in sharing and teaching on the steps to heal and unite fathers and their children while rebuilding healthy communication and renewed intimacy between a husband and wife. Don't miss this opportunity to read about methods that can reconcile conflicts relating to troubled kids in a confusing world. Dave offers a very raw and unabridged conversation that will bring simple and realistic methods for healing families.